Cover: The premises of the *Oslobodenje* newspaper,
Sarajevo, Summer 1998

French edition:

La paix séparée en ex-Yougoslavie

ISBN 92-871-3778-1

Edited by Sophie Jeleff, Council of Europe Publishing
Design: Council of Europe Publishing
Cover design: Graphic Design Workshop, Council of Europe
Cover photo: Louis Klipfel, Council of Europe

Council of Europe Publishing
F-67075 Strasbourg Cedex

ISBN 92-871-3780-3
© Council of Europe, December 1998
Printed in Belgium

A fractured peace: the former Yugoslavia

Debates

Parliamentary Assembly

Council of Europe Publishing

Founded in 1949, the **Council of Europe** is an intergovernmental organisation of forty member states.[1] Among its aims are: protecting and strengthening pluralist democracy and human rights, promoting the emergence of a genuine European cultural identity, seeking solutions to the problems facing society (the position of minorities, xenophobia and intolerance, environmental protection, bioethics, Aids, drugs, etc.), developing a political partnership with the new democracies of central and eastern Europe, and helping these same countries with their political, legislative and constitutional reforms.

The *Committee of Ministers* is the Council's decision-making body, made up of the foreign ministers of the forty member states or their permanent representatives. The consultative organ is the *Parliamentary Assembly* whose members are appointed by national parliaments. The *Congress of Local and Regional Authorities* of Europe is a consultative body representing local communities and regions.

The **Parliamentary Assembly** of the Council of Europe was the first European assembly to be created in the history of the continent. With delegations from forty national parliaments it is still the largest European assembly. The Assembly, which determines its own agenda, deals with current affairs and topical themes affecting society and international policy. It meets four times a year in the debating chamber of the *Palais de l'Europe* in plenary session open to the public. Its work has an important influence in determining the

---

1. Member states of the Council of Europe (at 1 December 1998): Albania, Andorra, Austria, Belgium, Bulgaria, Croatia, Cyprus, Czech Republic, Denmark, Estonia, Finland, France, Germany, Greece, Hungary, Iceland, Ireland, Italy, Latvia, Liechtenstein, Lithuania, Luxembourg, Malta, Moldova, Netherlands, Norway, Poland, Portugal, Romania, Russian Federation, San Marino, Slovak Republic, Slovenia, Spain, Sweden, Switzerland, "the former Yugoslav Republic of Macedonia", Turkey, Ukraine, United Kingdom.

activities of the Committee of Ministers. Matters discussed by the Parliamentary Assembly are also reported back by representatives to their national parliaments, and thus have an influence on governments.

Contents

War

From the outbreak of war
to the Dayton Agreements (1990-95)

The break-up of the Socialist Federative Republic of Yugoslavia (SFRY)

The events of the 1980s led to a revival of – sometimes extreme – nationalism within the constituent parts of the Socialist Federative Republic of Yugoslavia, as they did elsewhere in central and eastern Europe.

Mr Slobodan Milošević came to power in Belgrade in September 1987 as leader of the Serbian Communist Party. He exploited the political circumstances of the Socialist Federative Republic of Yugoslavia at the time, namely a deteriorating economy, an inefficient administration and a population which, under Tito, had not come to terms with the events of the second world war (because of highly biased historical accounts), in order to revive Serb nationalist feelings and fears, and to put an end to the autonomy of Vojvodina and Kosovo and proclaim their reunification with Serbia.

In February 1989, Mr Franjo Tudjman, after having become a symbol of national resistance to communism (for which he spent two terms in prison), founded the Croatian Democratic Union (HDZ). The party's nationalist platform, and use of old Croatian symbols, kindled local Serb fears – manipulated by Belgrade – of a revival of the Croatian fascist (Ustasha) state, which had existed during the second world war.

In June 1989, Mr Milošević delivered a major speech at Kosovo Polje, to mark the 600th anniversary of the battle against the Turks, deliberately leaving open the possibility of an armed struggle to achieve Serbian aims. Shortly afterwards, Serbs in Croatia demanded their own autonomous province.

These developments resulted in the end of the Yugoslav Communist Party in January 1990 when the Slovenian and Croatian delegations left its 14th Extraordinary Congress.

Croatia

Croatia, with an area of 56 538 km^2, had approximately 4 700 000 inhabitants before the war in 1991. About 78% of them were Croats and 12% (600 000) ethnic Serbs. Many other minorities were also present, but in relatively small numbers.

About half the Serb population lived in the border ("Krajina") area between Croatia and Bosnia and Herzegovina, which had also been the border between the Habsburg and Ottoman empires. In the period following the Serb defeat by the Turks in 1389 many Serbs moved north and were recruited by the Habsburg rulers as border troops.

Apart from settling in the Krajina (the mountainous area of Lika and East Dalmatia), Serbs settled in the Kordum and Banija regions (today also referred to as Northern Krajina) as well as in Western and Eastern Slavonia.

Croatia was the second richest and most developed area of the Socialist Federative Republic of Yugoslavia after Slovenia. It accounted for about one quarter of the country's gross social product (GSP), and industrial output.

In spring 1990, the first post-communist elections in Croatia saw the victory of the Croatian Democratic Union and Mr Franjo Tudjman was elected as President. Propaganda from Belgrade and the discriminatory policies as well as a general lack of understanding by the new Croatian authorities of the sensitivities of, particularly, the rural Serb population resulted in violent incidents in the Krajina in August 1990. The Yugoslav National Army (JNA), under Mr Milošević's control, prevented the Croatian authorities from restoring law and order.

In May 1991, Serb leaders prevented the Croatian Mr Stjepan Mesić, in accordance with the rotation procedure, from becoming Yugoslav President and Commander-in-Chief of the Yugoslav National Army.

Independence and war

The referendum held in Croatia on 19 May 1991 resulted in overwhelming support for independence. The outcome, however, was not accepted by leaders of the local Serb population, who proclaimed the independent "Republic of Serb Krajina" (RSK) and asked for unification with Serbia.

Croatia declared itself independent on 25 June 1991. Part of the Serb population began an armed rebellion, with the support of the Yugoslav National Army. Heavy fighting broke out in the region of Vukovar as well as in Pakrac. The Yugoslav navy shelled the Croatian coast including the medieval town of Dubrovnik. The newly-formed Croatian National Guard was at an enormous disadvantage vis-à-vis the professional Yugoslav National Army. The siege and the destruction of Vukovar in November 1991 proved to be a grim prelude of what was to follow in the coming years in Bosnia.

Croatia was recognised by Germany on 19 December 1991 and by the other members of the European Union on 15 January 1992. The European Union's efforts to obtain a ceasefire, however, proved fruitless. It was the United Nations Special Envoy, Mr Cyrus Vance, who obtained an agreement on 3 January 1992 which established a United Nations protection force (Unprofor) to facilitate demilitarisation of the area. It left about 23% of Croatian territory under control of the "Republic of Serb Krajina". The contested territories were divided into United Nations Protected Areas (UNPAs): Sector North (Northern Krajina); Sector South (Southern Krajina); Sector West (Western Slavonia) and Sector East (Eastern Slavonia).

Unprofor was given the following mandate: to supervise the ceasefire; to ensure the demilitarisation of the United Nations Protected Areas through the withdrawal of the Yugoslav National Army and the Croatian National Guard, as well as the disarmament of local Serb militia; to create the circumstances under which the demographic composition could be returned to pre-war conditions (that is, enable the return of displaced persons); to ensure the safety of the population by United Nations troops; to supervise the local police and to administer the UNPAs.

Although Unprofor managed to obtain a ceasefire and prevent further escalation of the fighting, it proved unable to carry out the other elements of its mandate. Although Croatian and JNA (Yugoslav National Army) forces left, the local Serb militia were not disarmed, and, instead of displaced persons being allowed to return, the remaining Croatian population was forced to leave.

As a result of the fighting and subsequent "ethnic cleansing", about 250 000 Croatian displaced persons had to seek refuge in Croatia. Nearly 3 000 persons were listed as missing.

Continued tension resulted in military operations such as the one which took place in January 1993 when Croatian forces successfully took the Maslenica Bridge and several other strategic areas from rebel Serb forces. A ceasefire agreement was only signed a year later by representatives of the Croatian Government and the "Republic of Serb Krajina" on 29 March 1994. The agreement foresaw an end to all hostilities, the withdrawal of heavy weapons from confrontation lines and the deployment of Unprofor troops in the area between the lines of separation. It also foresaw the establishment of joint commissions.

On 2 December 1994, an agreement was signed between Croatia and the "Republic of Serb Krajina", which foresaw the reopening of the Zagreb-Lipovac motorway and economic co-operation.

Following repeated earlier protests about Unprofor's inefficiency, President Tudjman announced, in January 1995, that Croatia would not accept the renewal of Unprofor's mandate. In a letter to the United Nations Secretary General of 12 January 1995, he stated that the continuous presence of Unprofor was "significantly counter-productive to the peace process" and mentioned that, despite its endeavours, Unprofor had been unable to implement the most important provisions of the Vance plan and subsequent United Nations Security Council resolutions. In particular it had failed to establish control of Croatia's international borders.

Widespread international pressure resulted in a joint statement by President Tudjman and United States Vice-President Gore in Copenhagen, on 12 March 1995, indicating Croatia's acceptance of a continued United Nations presence but with a new name and modified composition and mandate.

Following further negotiations, on 31 March 1995, the United Nations Security Council adopted Resolution 981 creating the United Nations Confidence Restoration Operation in Croatia (UNCRO), to consist of 8 750 UN peace keepers. The details of the operation, however, were not decided upon. Croatia in particular insisted that UNCRO's main task should be the control of Croatia's external borders. It also, initially, insisted that these troops only come from Nato countries, but dropped the latter demand in view of the UN's insistence on the multi-ethnic composition of its peace-keeping forces.

Western Slavonia

UNPA Sector West contained both Croats and Serbs with a confrontation line running through the middle of the sector. In addition, the municipality of Pakrac was divided into two parts (the "Pakrac pocket"). The Croatian army officially did not have forces in the area, although its special police are indistinguishable from regular army elite units. The Serbs did keep armed units in the UNPA. The Zagreb-Lipovac motorway was controlled by the Serbs.

The agreement referred to above included the re-opening of the motorway. However, incidents concerning the use of this motor-way resulted in several deaths and led to it being closed again by the Serb authorities at the end of April 1995.

Operation "Flash"

On 1 May 1995, at 5.30 a.m., the Croatian special police, sup-ported by artillery, began an operation to reopen the motorway. With the help of regular Croatian army forces, the operation was concluded on 2 May at 2 p.m. with the surrender of about 600 armed Serbs.

On 2 and 3 May, the "Republic of Serb Krajina" forces fired several rockets carrying cluster bombs on Zagreb, killing nine people and wounding nearly 200. Other Croatian towns such as Sisak, Karlovac, Novska, Nova Gradiška, Zupanja and Dubrovnik were shelled. The Croatian Government showed great restraint by not taking any retaliatory action.

Immediately after the military operation, Croatian forces arrested approximately 1 400 men (the data differ somewhat according to the sources) who were taken to different centres for screening. Most of these men were subsequently released, however without the International Committee of the Red Cross (ICRC) being notified.

Figures given by the Croat authorities concerning the number of Serb fighters killed (188) differ substantially from the figures given by the Serb representatives (400 killed). The Croatian authorities have stated that 127 casualties have been identified and that the process of identifying the others is continuing. International observers were not in a position to say which figures were exact.

Uncertainty also exists as to the fate of the wounded Serb fighters, reportedly numbering about 1 000. It would appear from information received from the International Committee of the Red Cross that a considerable number of wounded took refuge in Serb-held Bosnian territory and were treated in local hospitals there. About 11 000 civilians (according to ICRC data) left Western Slavonia in order to seek refuge in northern Bosnia and in Sector East. The United Nations High Commissioner for Refugees, which helped with the transport of many of these people, has been criticised for having acted too soon and having in fact contributed to an – unwanted – ethnic cleansing of Western Slavonia. Mr Akashi, Special Representative of the UN Secretary General, stressed that the United Nations agencies had been under enormous pressure from the "Republic of Serb Krajina" authorities, which threatened further attacks on Zagreb, to assist the Serb population in leaving the area.

About 2 000 Serbs are said to have remained in the area, mostly elderly people. A deep-seated mistrust *vis-à-vis* the Croatian authorities continues to exist, despite the latter's assurances, and it would seem that many Serbs do want to leave the area.

Of the Serbs who fled at the beginning of the fighting, 270 have made formal requests to return.

Bosnia and Herzegovina

On 3 March 1992, Bosnia and Herzegovina, ethnically the most complex republic (44% Muslim, 17% Croats, 31% Serbs) within the former Yugoslav Federation, declared its independence, following a referendum. On several occasions shots were fired at civilians by Serb irregulars. Soon afterwards, fighting erupted between rival Muslim and Croatian irregulars on the one hand and Yugoslav People's Army (YNA) troops and Serbian irregulars on the other. The main reason for the conflict has been the will of the Serbian community to maintain Bosnia and Herzegovina within the Yugoslav state.

Leaders of the three main ethnic groups signed an agreement on 18 March 1992, negotiated under the auspices of the European Community, on the future of the republic, which provided for its division into three autonomous units along ethnic lines. However, as violence continued to escalate, the agreement was abandoned.

On 6 April 1992, Bosnia and Herzegovina was recognised by the European Community, and on 22 May 1992 it was admitted to the United Nations. The Parliament of Bosnia and Herzegovina obtained Special Guest status with the Parliamentary Assembly of the Council of Europe on 29 January 1994. On 10 April 1995, Bosnia and Herzegovina applied for Council of Europe membership. The Committee of Ministers, on 12 September 1995, decided to consult the Parliamentary Assembly.

Although a formal alliance, and several agreements were concluded between Croatia and Bosnia and Herzegovina in July 1992, the situation on the ground between Bosnian Croats and Muslims rapidly deteriorated. A bitter war ensued, dramatically symbolised by the destruction of Mostar and its world famous Old Bridge. The Bosnian Croats proclaimed their own state of Herceg-Bosna. This entity was mainly supported by the Croats living in Herzegovina.

These events gave rise to grave concern. The fear was voiced that a deal had been made between Croatia and Serbia to divide Bosnia. The Council of Europe's Parliamentary Assembly joined most western governments in putting pressure on both sides to end this conflict. The realisation by both parties that the Serbs were the main problem, as well as a desire not to alienate the west, resulted in two separate agreements signed in March 1994 in Washington. One established a confederation between Bosnia and Herzegovina and Croatia. The second set up a Croatian-Muslim federation within Bosnia and Herzegovina itself.

According to the Croat Government the existence of two entities, namely the Republic and the Federation of Bosnia and Herzegovina, and the resulting institutional difficulties also had to be taken into account. Following the Serb conquest of the United Nations Protected Areas of Srebnica and Zepa and the combined offensive of "Republic of Serb Krajina" and Bosnian Forces against the Bihac enclave in July 1995, an agreement was signed by President Tudjman of Croatia, President Izetbegović of the Republic of Bosnia and Herzegovina and Mr Zubac, President of the Federation of Bosnia and Herzegovina on 22 July 1995. It guaranteed military assistance by Croatia and co-operation between the Croatian army, the army of Bosnia and Herzegovina and the Croatian Defence Council (HVO) – the Bosnian Croat forces.

Operation "Storm"

At the beginning of August 1995, Croatia launched a massive military attack in UNPA Sectors North and South and these areas were brought under Croatian Government control. The Croatian decision to use military force must also be seen in the light of the failure of the international community to protect the population of "safe areas" in Bosnia and Herzegovina.

The Croat action caused a massive flow of Serb refugees, number-ing between 150 000 and 200 000, to Serb-held Bosnian territory and to Serbia proper. There have been reports of these refugees having come under attack by the Croatian army, as well as by Croatian civilians.

In retaliation, Croats were driven out of areas held by the Bosnian Serbs. However, the events also increased pressure on the Bosnian Serbs to accept a political solution to the conflict.

In accordance with the decisions of the London Conference of 22 July 1995, to ensure the protection of all the United Nations "safe areas", Nato planes and the UN Rapid Reaction Force attacked Bosnian Serb military targets at the end of August, after a mortar attack on Sarajevo which left over thirty people dead.

On 8 September 1995, a ministerial conference between the parties to the conflict resulted in a set of agreed basic principles (see appendix below).

The Nato strike lasted until 20 September. Up to that date, regular Croatian Army units and the HVO, as well as the Bosnian Army had made substantial territorial gains in Western Bosnia, at the expense of Bosnian Serb forces.

Agreement draws nearer

On 10 October 1995, following pressure from the United States, a ceasefire was signed, and an international conference was organ-ised for the end of October in the United States in Dayton (Ohio), with the three presidents: Alija Izetbegović, Slobodan Milošević and Franjo Tudjman. The Dayton Agreements, which were signed on 21 November 1995, were to bring about the end of the war, unite Bosnia and Herzegovina and lift the sanctions against the Federal Republic of Yugoslavia.

Appendix

Agreed basic principles (8 September 1995)[1]

1. Bosnia and Herzegovina will continue in legal existence with its present borders and continuing international recognition.

2. Bosnia and Herzegovina will consist of two entities, the Federation of Bosnia and Herzegovina as established by the Washington Agreements, and the Republika Srpska.

2.1. The 51 :49 parameter of the territorial proposal of the contact group is the basis for a settlement. This territorial proposal is open for adjustment by mutual agreement.

2.2. Each entity will continue to exist under its present constitution (amended to accommodate these basic principles).

2.3. Both entities will have the right to establish parallel special relationships with neighbouring countries, consistent with the sovereignty and territorial integrity of Bosnia and Herzegovina.

2.4. The two entities will enter into reciprocal commitments:

a. to hold complete elections under international auspices;

b. to adopt and adhere to normal international human rights standards and obligations to allow freedom of movement and enable displaced persons to repossess their homes or receive just compensation;

c. to engage in binding arbitration to resolve disputes between them.

---

1. The basic principles were agreed upon by Mr Muhamed Sacirbey, Foreign Minister of the Republic of Bosnia and Herzegovina (Bosnia and Herzegovina), Mr Mate Granić, Foreign Minister of the Republic of Croatia (Croatia) and Mr Milan Milutinović, Foreign Minister of the Federal Republic of Yugoslavia (Yugoslavia), and witnessed by Representatives of France, Germany, Russia, the United Kingdom and the United States, and by the European Union Special Negotiator for the Former Yugoslavia.

3. The entities have agreed in principle to the following:

3.1. The appointment of a Commission for Displaced Persons authorised to enforce (with assistance from international entities) the obligations of both entities to enable displaced persons to repossess their homes or receive just compensation.

3.2. The establishment of a Bosnia and Herzegovina Human Rights Commission, to enforce the entities' human rights obligations. The two entities will abide by the commission's decisions.

3.3. The establishment of a joint Bosnia and Herzegovina public corporation, financed by the two entities, to the benefit of both entities.

3.4. The appointment of a commission to preserve national monuments.

3.5. The design and implementation of a system of arbitration for the solution of disputes between the two entities.

During the conflict: humanitarian aid and embargoes

The invaluable work done by organisations such as the Office of the United Nations High Commissioner for Refugees, the International Committee of the Red Cross, Unicef and the humanitarian non-governmental organisations was constantly hampered, if not rendered impossible. Humanitarian action is the expression of a form of solidarity which sometimes comes too late. It is highly reliant on voluntary funding, which is invariably insufficient to deal with the actual needs encountered. The Unicef budget, for instance, comes solely from voluntary contributions made by governments and the public via sales of greetings cards and other products; despite repeated requests by the organisation, only 22% of the funds currently needed for children in the former Yugoslavia were available.

European contributions to the HCR had still not come through by mid-1993; in August it told the press that it had only US$ 162.8 million at its disposal, whereas it would need US$ 420 million to cover needs up to the end of the year; similarly, *Médecins sans frontières* reported a drop in subsidies from the European Community and blamed the over-strict conditions to be fulfilled in order to qualify for them.

The economic difficulties facing neighbouring countries which took in refugees lessened the sympathy felt for them, and consequently offers of accommodation and assistance to refugees decreased.

The embargo imposed on Serbia and Montenegro had terrible consequences for the health and nutrition of the most vulnerable groups of civilians, and a number of humanitarian concessions had to be made to avoid these consequences, which were not the purpose of the embargo.

On-the-ground protection was usually necessary to enable the soldiers to get supplies and medicines through to those whose survival depended on them. Where operations aimed at evacuating civilians, women and children were possible, they were carried out under dangerous conditions and were therefore criticised, sometimes because the whole underlying principle was felt to be wrong.

Some controversial attempts to evacuate the injured prompted disputes about the number of persons involved and the criterion for the choice of evacuees. During "Operation Irma" in August 1993, the sudden frantic competition between governments to offer treatment seemed to have more to do with a political and media operation than with humanitarian relief. Moreover, the press passed on allegations about bureaucracy and the excessive length of time taken to reach and implement decisions. Even the humanitarian organisations mentioned the lack of policy guidelines and confusion.

This begged the question of what practical arrangements were needed to achieve optimum effectiveness in, and co-ordination of, humanitarian action. European public opinion was in very broad agreement that such action was needed, and could not understand the hesitations and hitches, which they considered to be the fault of the politicians.

The conflict in the former Yugoslavia has clearly shown that the issue of humanitarian action in time of war must be treated separately from disaster relief. Even if such action must ultimately remain the responsibility of the competent international organisations and

NGOs, this conflict demonstrated that European governments must be involved and that a concerted strategy for humanitarian action is sadly lacking.

Embargo: sanctions against the Federal Republic of Yugoslavia (Serbia and Montenegro)

In September 1991 the United Nations Security Council expressed deep concern at the fighting in the former Yugoslavia, which at that time was taking place in Croatia, and determined that the situation there constituted a threat to international peace and security. As part of the efforts of the international community to stop the fighting and loss of human life, and to assist the collective efforts for bringing peace to the area so that dialogue between the warring sides could lead to a durable solution to the conflict, the United Nations Security Council decided to impose economic sanctions in three main consecutive stages.

First stage (September 1991-March 1992): on 25 September 1991 the United Nations Security Council passed Resolution 713.

- The resolution imposed a general and complete embargo on all deliveries of weapons and military equipment to "Yugoslavia" (paragraph 6).
- The resolution aimed mainly to ensure observance of the cease-fire agreements of 17 and 22 September between the Serbs and the Croatians. It urgently appealed to and encouraged all parties to reach such a settlement through negotiation at the conference on Yugoslavia and its mechanisms (paragraph 5), launched by the European Union and its member states with the support of the states participating in the Conference on Security and Co-operation in Europe (CSCE).

Two months later – on 15 December 1991 – the Security Council passed Resolution 724, by which it established a committee of the

Security Council on the sanctions under Resolution 713, to monitor compliance with the arms embargo and to recommend appropriate measures so that it was effectively applied.

The second stage (May 1992-April 1993): on 30 May 1992 Resolution 757 was passed.

- The resolution introduced a broad range of trade and economic sanctions against the Federal Republic of Yugoslavia (Serbia and Montenegro), spelt out in detail in the resolution's points 4 to 9, which may be summarised as follows:

  - an import prohibition against commodities and products originating in the Federal Republic of Yugoslavia;

  - a prohibition on the "sale and supply" to any person or body in the Federal Republic of Yugoslavia or for the purpose of any business carried on in or from the Federal Republic of Yugoslavia;

  - a requirement that all states deny take-off, landing and over-flight to aircraft destined for or taking off from the territory of the Federal Republic of Yugoslavia.

- In paragraph 6 the resolution stated that the prohibitions did not apply to the trans-shipment through the Federal Republic of Yugoslavia of commodities and products originating outside it, and that the Committee on Sanctions of the Security Council would approve guidelines for effecting such trans-shipments.

- The immediate purpose of the new sanctions was to ensure the implementation of a new ceasefire agreement of 12 April 1992 to stop the fighting in Bosnia and Herzegovina, and to prevent continuation of the persistent ceasefire violations in Croatia.

- The resolution, having established "that in the very complex context of events (...) all parties bear some responsibility for the situation", again expressed support for the efforts through the conference on Yugoslavia to reach a negotiated political solution in the area.

A partial ban on trans-shipments was introduced six months later under Resolution 787 of 16 November 1992.

Third stage (since April 1993): the United Nations Security Council adopted Resolution 820 on 17 April 1993.

- The resolution imposed tough new sanctions against the Federal Republic of Yugoslavia, listed in detail in paragraphs 12 to 39, which may be summarised as follows:
  - a complete prohibition on unauthorised trans-shipment of goods through the Federal Republic of Yugoslavia;
  - special authorisation and monitoring of trans-shipments on the Danube;
  - freezing of funds belonging to authorities or undertakings in the Federal Republic of Yugoslavia, held by states, persons or entities implementing the resolutions of the United Nations;
  - a ban on passage of freight vehicles and rolling stock into or out of the Federal Republic of Yugoslavia except at a strictly limited number of road and rail border crossing points to be approved by the Committee on Sanctions.

- The immediate objective of the new tightening of the sanctions was to ensure adoption of the Vance-Owen peace plan for Bosnia and Herzegovina, by making the Bosnian Serbs accept its provisions, the other two sides to the conflict having agreed to support the plan. Paragraph 31 of Resolution 820 expresses the readiness of the Security Council to review and gradually lift all the measures contained in its resolution, if there is verified evidence that the Bosnian Serb party is co-operating in good faith in effective implementation of the plan.

Consequences and problems for neighbouring countries

Compliance with the embargo against Serbia and Montenegro has had serious consequences for the neighbouring countries, and especially for the front-line states. In connection with the sanctions, requests for consultations under Article 50 and for compensation of economic losses have been deposited at the United Nations by Bulgaria, Hungary, Romania, Slovakia and Ukraine.

Consideration of the consequences and problems for the countries affected should have as its point of departure an awareness of the general conditions prevailing in most of them, including virtually all of the front-line states on the eve of sanctions in 1991 and 1992. The economies were experiencing a severe transitional recession of much greater depth and severity than initially anticipated. The recession had been brought about both by the sudden loss of vitally important markets in the former Soviet Union, as well as by the abrupt collapse of internal demand as a result of "shock therapy" policies undertaken in most of the countries to deal with excess purchasing power.

Of course, the underlying causes of the deep economic crises in these countries were rooted in the low efficiency and serious misallocation of resources inherited from the past, making fundamental structural adjustment all the more urgent. The imposition of sanctions at that particular moment of the transition process inevitably made the task of adjustment incomparably more difficult. It should also be remembered that a number of these countries had already suffered major losses as a result of United Nations sanctions against Iraq and also against Libya, for which no compensation was forthcoming.

The embargo provoked a general disruption of initial supply-side responses to stabilisation policies and efforts at economic revival – due to the disruption or severance of transportation links to remaining external markets (which had acquired new importance following the dissolution of Comecon) and the resulting drastic decreases in export revenue, resource availability, output and employment.

Neighbouring countries registered lasting losses of external market shares owing to disruptions to market access by exporters to markets in central and western Europe and in the Middle East, due to the sanctions.

Severe disturbances were also caused to the newly established domestic markets and market structures in most of the countries concerned – as a result of the particular difficulties that emerging private companies experienced due to the sanctions. To this should be added the strong boost to black market practices and profiteering in conditions of constricted supplies.

Substantial additional costs were incurred as a result of the requirements to ensure the strict observance of sanctions – such as the maintenance of additional customs and police personnel and facilities. Damage due to vessels being detained for inspection and verification of ownership or cargo destinations ran into millions of US dollars.

The expected arrival of a significant influx of refugees has caused considerable social and economic problems.

Finally, the degree of confidence on the part of the international investment community in the perspectives offered by these countries suffered perceptibly. Investor interest waned while waiting for more stable and predictable conditions.

The cumulative effect of these consequences and problems was such as to lead inevitably to an erosion of the overall national security of the countries affected. It must be remembered that the region in which the sanctions were applied remained one of the major points of acute international tension, and that almost every country there faced the overriding need to redefine its national security precepts and to seek new guarantees.

Of the greatest urgency among these problems was the problem of transportation and communications – in view of the fact that the territories of Serbia and Montenegro lie across the principal land and Danube river routes through Europe and into the Middle East. The ban on transit through these territories caused a number of severe logistical problems:

– trade flows were severed, with all the ensuing consequences for fulfilment of contracts, preserving the good condition of merchandise, and so on. Shipments had to be rerouted, which proved to be extremely complicated due to the underdeveloped infrastructure in the area and the difficult terrain;

– this in turn created severe bottlenecks at critical border crossings along the Danube and into the areas of central Europe and the Mediterranean. The re-routing affected the shipment of perishable goods, significantly increased transportation costs and affected competitiveness;

– unfortunately, the customs and border authorities in some of the countries adjacent to the sanctions enforcement area chose to introduce punitive increases in border taxes. In other cases it became virtually standard practice to extort illegal payment in order to cross congested checkpoints;

– the transport companies in the neighbouring countries saw their businesses decline drastically, and this at a time when they had been experiencing the full impact of the deep recession in the area and were struggling to restructure and streamline operations. This was all the more serious since in many of these countries international road, rail and river transport had grown into a major source of employment and foreign currency income.

Public opinion in many of these countries increasingly came to view the economic and also the broader consequences of the sanctions – which they endured without any material compensation for the losses suffered – as a wholly unjustified "surcharge" for membership in the international community. Obviously, such a setting provided multiple opportunities for swaying official policies and voter preferences away from the determined pursuit of pluralist institution-building and market-based development.

Finally, a word must be said regarding the special suffering on the part of the peoples of Serbia and Montenegro. The full force of hardship flowing from the sanctions was borne by innocent civilians in these countries, with little or no say as to the policies and practices of the governing bodies in the Federal Republic of Yugoslavia.

Human rights violations

Massive violations

As soon as the massive and flagrant violations of human rights in the territory of the former Yugoslavia came to light in the course of the summer of 1992, they caused such a justifiable and necessary outcry that various international bodies – both worldwide and European – took initiatives to attempt to end the conflict, to allow humanitarian aid to reach the intended recipients, but also to provide legal means of action and to advocate the prosecution of war criminals.

Nationalism and xenophobia have had free rein in the former Yugoslavia and endangered human rights to a degree not witnessed in western Europe since the end of the second world war.

The civilian population was a prime target of the warring parties. "Ethnic cleansing" operations were often carried out by paramilitary groups bearing little resemblance to a regular army.

It is generally accepted that these practices were, for the most part, attributable to the Serb forces, who were also the first to use them. Nevertheless, it is likely that the other parties in the conflict also, to a lesser extent, used similar tactics.

The systematic rape of women belonging to minority groups as a means of destroying these minorities represented a new kind of war crime.

The parties in the conflict did not respect the rules recognised as being part of the laws of war. In the face of these barbaric and systematic violations of humanitarian law, the 1949 Geneva Convention relative to the Protection of Civilian Persons in Time of War and its 1977 Additional Protocols conveys a feeling of unreality: virtually all the protective provisions were violated.

Among the elementary humanitarian principles which were deliberately flouted and violated was the principle to the effect that children should be involved neither passively nor actively in warfare. As early as 1924 the League of Nations approved a declaration on the rights of the child which stipulated that children must be the first to receive relief in situations of distress and stated that men and women of all nations recognised that mankind must give children the best it could offer.

During the conflict in the former Yugoslavia more than seventeen of the forty-one articles in the first part of the Convention were violated. Articles 38 and 39 lays down the principle of the protection of children in situations of war.

Children were the victims of summary executions, were systematically targeted, killed and wounded, often to serve as bait so that adults coming to help them could be shot down.

Social institutions, including hospitals and schools, were targeted for purposes of warfare and destruction. A prime objective of international co-operation must be to reconstruct these and restore them to an operational state. In recent armed conflicts women and children have increasingly been used as human shields, and there is also increasing use of antipersonnel mines which look like, and are the same colour as, toys – and children are, of course, the prime victims.

It was said that about 60 000 antipersonnel mines per week were being spread around the territory in the formerYugoslavia. Children were particularly hard hit by the deprivation of, or difficulties in obtaining, food and water and the lack of heating, not to mention the difficulties in receiving adequate medical treatment and care. Children in Sarajevo had to subsist mainly on bread, rice and pasta.

Violence, terror and collective madness became the children's everyday environment. Not only did they suffer barbaric acts, they also witnessed them. In the republics of the former Yugoslavia approximately one million children are suffering from psychological trauma and 150 000 children and their parents have been directly exposed to terror for long periods. The symptoms of post-trauma stress are: guilt about having survived; depression and anxiety; inability to imagine any future; irritability and miscellaneous psychosomatic disorders and symptoms. The individual bears the psychological scars for years, hence the need to set up psychological support services without delay.

The collective rape of women and children, which was used as a weapon of ethnic and cultural destruction, elicited the unanimous indignation of the international community. The Assembly must endorse the judgment given by the Committee of Ministers of the Council of Europe, which declared that rape "is a violation of human rights and (...) the use of rape as an instrument of warfare and within the context of a strategy of ethnic cleansing is a war crime and should be considered as a crime against humanity".

The indignation and outrage at such crimes as well as the "ethnic cleansing" issue were to some extent addressed by the decision taken in February 1993 by the United Nations Security Council to set up the International Criminal Tribunal for the Former Yugoslavia to consider the violations of international humanitarian law.

Like many wars, the one in the former Yugoslavia has been marked by the handing down of hatred from generation to generation.

Dr Samir Basta quoted the example of young boys from the Middle East who, whatever their religion, are taught by their mothers from their earliest infancy to speak in a war-like, aggressive manner and hate the enemy, and are indoctrinated to become warriors or martyrs.

Rejecting a fratricidal war

Considerable numbers of deserters and draft resisters refused to take part in a fratricidal, nationalist war. Estimates vary between 100 000 according to the Anti-War Centre in Belgrade and 300 000 according to "Women in Black", from the Federal Republic of Yugoslavia, Bosnia and Herzegovina and Croatia.

A statement by the Office for Hungarians Living Abroad confirmed the tactics used by the Serbs to encourage Hungarians to leave Vojvodina: "One of the most striking examples consisted in enlisting young men in the Yugoslav army".[1]

Methods of enlistment of young people into the Yugoslav army became widespread during the conflict, as did violations of the right to object to military service on grounds of conscience as a legitimate exercise of the right to freedom of thought, conscience and religion and, especially under the circumstances, of the right to refuse service in those elements of the military forces responsible for "ethnic cleansing" and other grave violations of human rights in Croatia and Bosnia and Herzegovina. Soldiers from Montenegro were forced to fight with the Bosnian Serb forces, but there were also reports of Croats being forcibly enlisted to fight in Bosnia and Herzegovina. Most of these were persons with dual Croat-Bosnian nationality or Croats born in Bosnia and Herzegovina.

------

1. See the Council of Europe Parliamentary Assembly's report on the situation of the refugees and displaced persons in Serbia, Montenegro and "the former Yugoslav Republic of Macedonia" (Doc. 6910).

Refugees from Bosnia and Herzegovina in the Federal Republic of Yugoslavia, some as young as sixteen, were also forcibly enlisted. Many young men deserted to avoid conscription; if captured, they were subjected to very severe measures.

Many of the refugees in other European countries, particularly in Council of Europe member states, would run the risk of being forcibly conscripted into the armed forces if they were returned to Croatia, Serbia or Montenegro.

Forcible conscription took place in the Federal Republic of Yugoslavia; it mainly affected members of minorities such as Muslims from the Sandjak area, Gypsies, Hungarians from Vojvodina and Albanians from Kosovo, as well as Serbs, many of whom refused to take part in the war.

In Croatia, refugees of Croatian origin who were forced to flee areas of Bosnia and Herzegovina when they were occupied by the Serbs or Muslims were returned to Bosnia, where they faced forcible conscription. Croatian refugees from the Krajina, particularly those born in Bosnia and Herzegovina, or to Croatian citizens of Serbian origin, met with the same fate.

Finally, the right to object to military service on conscientious grounds was not recognised in practice in either the Federal Republic of Yugoslavia or Croatia, even though it was enshrined in law. The Croatian Constitution provided for alternative non-combatant service but only within the framework of military activities.

Situation from the legal viewpoint

Although the Yugoslav Constitution provided for conscientious objection to military service as an expression of the right to freedom of thought, conscience and religion, the implementing regulations were not adopted and a refusal to serve in the armed forces was punishable by up to twenty years' imprisonment under Section 214 of the Yugoslav Criminal Code. This section covered all Yugoslav citizens who avoided fighting in the war by going abroad and staying there. Proceedings were instituted against an estimated 15 000 to 20 000 individuals.

In Croatia the problem mainly affected refugees from Bosnia and Herzegovina who were sent back there and forcibly enlisted. Deserters who were deported faced not merely a court case and five years' imprisonment, but might be subjected to physical abuse by paramilitary forces or ultra-nationalist groups, discrimination (loss of job or housing, administrative problems), and so on or their families might be subjected to harassment.

Situation from the ethical viewpoint

The young men labelled as deserters or draft resisters were actually people who refused to take part in atrocities such as ethnic cleansing – in other words, men who took steps to ensure that they did not become war criminals liable to appear before the international court for serious violations of international humanitarian law.

Tens of thousands of deserters and draft resisters sought refuge in member states, which generally granted them temporary, precarious protection.

Virtually without exception, the member states did not consider desertion as grounds for granting asylum, and indeed their applications were often rejected as "manifestly unfounded", even though the Office of the United Nations Hight Commissioner for Refugees' *Handbook on procedures and criteria for determining refugee status* states that "where, however, the type of military action, with which an individual does not wish to be associated, is condemned by the international community as contrary to basic rules of human conduct, punishment for desertion or draft evasion could, in the light of all other requirements of the definition, in itself be regarded as persecution".

Peace and human rights

Agreement on Human Rights (Annexe 6 of the Dayton Agreements) – Nature of protection

According to both the Constitution of Bosnia and Herzegovina (Article II, paragraph 1) and the Agreement on Human Rights (Article I), Bosnia and Herzegovina and the two entities (the Federation of Bosnia and Herzegovina and the Republika Srpska) guarantee to all persons within their jurisdiction "the highest level of internationally recognised human rights and fundamental freedoms", including those set forth in the European Convention on Human Rights (ECHR) and its protocols and other international agreements listed in the appendix to the constitution and the agreement. Among those agreements, there are three other Council of Europe conventions: the European Convention on the Prevention of Torture and Inhuman or Degrading Treatment or Punishment; the European Charter for Regional or Minority Languages and the Framework Convention for the Protection of National Minorities.

The rights and freedoms secured by the European Convention on Human Rights shall apply directly in Bosnia and Herzegovina and have priority over all other law (Article II, paragraph 2 of the constitution). This means that even without (or prior to) ratification by Bosnia and Herzegovina (which could only be made after its accession to the Council of Europe) the substantive part of the European Convention on Human Rights is fully and directly applicable as part of the constitution.

With regard to the other three Council of Europe conventions, the constitution provides that Bosnia and Herzegovina shall become a party (Article II, paragraph 7). In this respect it is important to be aware of the following problems which could arise in the implementation of this clause and which the Committee of Ministers of the Council of Europe will have to face:

- the European Convention on the Prevention of Torture and Inhuman or Degrading Treatment or Punishment is not open for signature to non-member states of the Council of Europe (except on the basis of its Protocol No. 1 which is not included in the list appended to the constitution and the agreements and, in any case, is not put into force);

- the European Charter for Regional or Minority Languages is open for signature to non-member states of the Council of Europe following its entry into force on 1 March 1998;

The Framework Convention for the Protection of National Minorities, however, allows for non-member states to be invited to accede even before its entry into force and, therefore, is the only convention to which Bosnia and Herzegovina could immediately become party upon request.

Substantive human rights provisions

The Dayton Agreements had the merit of stopping the fighting and giving cause for some optimism. This does not mean that human rights abuses stopped.

"The highest level of internationally recognised human rights and fundamental freedoms" was secured, according to Appendix 6 of the Dayton Agreements, to all persons within the jurisdiction of the parties, including the rights and freedoms provided in the European Convention on Human Rights and its protocols and other human rights agreements. Nevertheless, the problem still remained whether the people of Bosnia and Herzegovina would be able to realise their human rights and fundamental freedoms, such as freedom of movement, freedom of expression, choice of place of residence, work, regardless of their different ethnic origin.

Right to life

Apart from the incidents of killings and sniping which were still being reported, even after the war, there was also the problem of the estimated 3 million mines strewn across innumerable locations throughout the country. A great number of unmarked mines still pose a continuing threat to the lives of civilians.

Right to liberty and security of person

The parties failed to comply entirely with the Dayton provision regarding release of prisoners. By 14 March 1996 nearly 800 prisoners had been freed while it was thought that more than 200 persons remained in detention, including some sixty suspected war criminals.

Freedom of movement

Freedom of movement for the citizens of Bosnia and Herzegovina improved substantially following the signing of the Dayton Agreements. Nevertheless, their ability to move safely throughout the country is still greatly restricted.

Progress was made, mainly in and around the city of Sarajevo. However, incidents in early 1996 in which travellers were stopped and detained by opposing factions around Sarajevo show that the situation was still precarious at that time.

With regard to Mostar, freedom of movement between East and West Mostar was guaranteed in theory, but hardly at all in practice. This issue has been one of the most difficult ones faced by the city's European Union Administration and has marked the failure of the two partners in the Federation of Bosnia and Herzegovina to achieve meaningful unification.

Some slight improvement took place with regard to freedom of movement in areas near inter-entity boundary lines. Nevertheless, movements from one entity to another remained infrequent.

Freedom of expression

This freedom, and in particular freedom of the media, was a precondition of free and fair elections.

All sides used the media to advocate national and religious hatred and incite discrimination. For the integrity of Bosnia and Herzegovina to be preserved, much effort had to be made in this area. The use of the media to favour one nationality at the expense of the others marked the disputes that occurred over the transfer of Serb-held suburbs of Sarajevo to the federation and continued to be the case in Mostar and in Herzeg-Bosna where only Croatian television programmes were transmitted.

The lack of an opposition press in the Republika Srpska was evident, as were the difficulties of a non-governmental enterprise, Studio 99, in obtaining a broadcasting licence in Sarajevo.

Much freedom of the media in Bosnia Herzegovina and in the two entities depended on the exercise of such a freedom in neighbouring countries.

Freedom from discrimination

Discrimination in access to housing, employment, education, medical and other services on the basis of ethnic origin continued to be practised in both entities and constituted one of the main threats to a lasting peace.

The work of the Office of the Ombudspersons for the Federation of Bosnia and Herzegovina has been significant in documenting and addressing allegations of discrimination, but government authorities were often unco-operative in responding to the ombudspersons' findings.

Respect for human rights in Bosnia and Herzegovina was fundamental to the free and fair conduct of elections. Without freedom of expression, and in particular of the media, for instance, how could the elections be considered "free and fair?"

The electoral system provided by Dayton defined eligibility for the presidency of Bosnia and Herzegovina according to candidates' nationality. This provision as well as others in the agreement making nationality-based distinctions were regrettable, since concessions to expediency could harden into permanently impenetrable barriers between Bosnians of different nationalities.

War and the media

The media operating on the territory of the former Yugoslavia shared responsibility for the origin and development of the conflicts raging there, and also played a central role in the resolution of those same conflicts. The chances of lasting peace in the region require the existence, among other things, of the free circulation of information and of independent media.

The violation of the rights of journalists, infringements of the principle of independence of the media and the shortage of material led to a situation that can be described as disastrous: the use of state television for propaganda was a fact in Croatia, Bosnia and Herzegovina and Serbia; all forms of Albanian language media were closed down in Kosovo; the press became less and less pluralist in Croatia; and the war in Bosnia and Herzegovina forced journalists to risk their lives in an attempt to continue to circulate information.

During a hearing which took place in Strasbourg in 1993 with journalists from most countries of the former Yugoslavia and representatives of non-governmental organisations, it appeared that the basic political and professional background was very much the same in Bosnia and Herzegovina, Croatia and Serbia, with television tightly controlled by the authorities and used by those in power to broadcast "nationalism and hate" in order to maintain a climate of war over their respective populations. This was all the more serious as television was the only medium available for the great majority of the population.

According to a journalist from Sarajevo, recognition by the international community of the ultra-nationalist political leaders rather than of the democratic institutions reinforced the power of the government-controlled media. Participants at the hearing voiced a certain disillusion and distrust in the international community, and in particular in European organisations. However, journalists from the former Yugoslavia present at the hearing realised that the situation, which was difficult enough for them to understand, would be incomprehensible for most western Europeans.

The situation of the media mid-war[1]

Slovenia

The public broadcasting body, Radiotelevizja Slovenija, was managed by a board of directors appointed by the parliament. There was a national television station, supported by taxes and advertisements, a small private television station, Kanal A Ljubljana, three national radio programmes of Radio Slovenija and twenty-two local radio stations. There were six national daily newspapers with a circulation of around 250 000 (Slovenia has a population of 1.9 million) and some forty-five magazines. No major problems

1. This section is based on reports by Mr Mazowiecki (Special Rapporteur of the United Nations Human Rights Commission) to a meeting convened by the Secretary General of the Council of Europe (Strasbourg, March 1993) and to the Steering Committee on the Mass Media (CDMM) seminar on the media in situations of conflict and tension (Strasbourg, 29 November-1 December 1993); a report by *Reporters sans frontières* (October 1993); the hearing on the situation of the media in the former Yugoslavia (Strasbourg, 15 October 1993); a report on Freedom of the media in eastern Europe and in the countries of the former Soviet Union by the Trans-Atlantic Dialogue on European Broadcasting (second edition, November 1993); the *Directory of indigenous non-governmental organisations and independent media in the former Yugoslavia* established by the Institute for War and Peace Reporting; *The struggle for independent media in ex-Yugoslavia*, prepared by the Ljubljana Co-ordinating Centre; and other material from the former Yugoslavia.

have been reported in the field of the media in Slovenia, in particular when compared with other countries in the region. Ljubljana was chosen for the seat of the Co-ordinating Centre for Independent Media.

Croatia

After two years of war a clear picture of the Croatian media had emerged. In 1993 there was not a single important newspaper or television or radio station that did not belong to or was not controlled by the state or the ruling party (Croatian Democratic Union – HDZ). The process started with the "privatisation" of the two major daily newspapers, most of the shares in which were owned by the state or leading Croatian Democratic Union figures. The last to fall was *Slobodna Dalmacija* in October 1992. A systematic cleansing of all journalists that did not support Croatian Democratic Union policies ensued.

The law on private radio and television was about to be adopted but independent journalists feared that it might confirm state control. There were five local television stations with varying degrees of independence (in Zagreb, Split, Osijek, Èacovek and Opuzen) and some small independent local radio stations, but their influence could not be compared to that of the state-controlled radio and television. The project Radio Rijeka/Fiume International, now Radio Lungomare, launched with the support of the Council of Europe in February 1992, waited for months for a reply to its request for a broadcasting licence; yet, a radio project of the ruling party received its licence in a short period of time. The national news agency, Hina, was closely controlled by the government party – the Croatian Democratic Union (HDZ) – and there was a virtual state monopoly in press, printing and distribution.

The Croat Government used the media for propaganda. The war could not be brought to an end until television, radio and newspapers stopped "inciting hate". According to the Chairman of the Croatian Helsinki Committee for Human Rights, "the state television created an atmosphere of justified arrogance. The state-controlled media adopted a collective madness of hate speech and the population lived in a permanent state of fear". The newspaper *Hrvatska Vjesnik*, for instance, was said to glorify the war and to carry the most bestial, racist, anti-Serb and anti-Muslim propaganda. Nothing was done to prevent this, whereas the pacifist newspaper *Arkzin* was considered to be anti-Croatian.

Physical and psychological aggression were used to intimidate all opposition to the regime and those not unconditionally in favour were considered to be against it. Two journalists were arrested in October 1993 in connection with a bomb explosion in Split, and another journalist was detained for not turning up in court. The twenty-person Croatian Helsinki Committee for Human Rights came under constant attack.

An additional problem was the price of newspapers, especially because of the difficult economic situation. Thus a daily newspaper cost the price of a loaf of bread, and monthly salaries were about 200 Deutschmarks. The number of copies of each newspaper fell steadily, and the influence of state television grew accordingly.

Bosnia and Herzegovina

The situation in Bosnia and Herzegovina in 1993 was similar to that in Croatia, with the state-controlled media producing enormous amounts of hate and hysteria. It should not be forgotten that the war started with the occupation of nine out of the eleven television transmitters and that propaganda was essential to the continuation of hostilities. There were three television channels in Bosnia and Herzegovina, all controlled by the ethnic party in power: BiHTV Mostar (Sarajevo) broadcasting for Muslims, SRT (Pale) for Serbs and TV Mostar for Croats; there were also independent television stations in Bugojno, Tuzla, Zenica and Konjić.

After 500 days of combat in Sarajevo, during which five journalists were killed and thirty wounded, the newspaper *Oslobodenje* found itself in serious difficulty. In mid-October 1993 its main problem was how to get fuel for its electricity generator. Fuel was available on the black market, but unaffordable, and the Bosnian Government was not prepared to help, as *Oslobodenje* remained an independent paper. The European Union claims to have given 3.8 million ecus to independent media in the former Yugoslavia, including *Oslobodenje*, but not all of the money reached them. The International Federation of Journalists (IFJ) and the International Federation of Newspaper Publishers (FIEJ), supported the independent media and co-ordinated material support. The Office of the United Nations High Commissioner for Refugees (UNHCR) had difficulties handling this through its own channels. The only means of communication with the outside world was through radio amateurs. In western Europe *Oslobodenje* was Bosnia and Herzegovina's best-known media outlet, but the IFJ pointed out that this was not the only newspaper in Sarajevo, nor the most important and many people considered it less than independent. According to the Ljubljana Co-ordinating Centre the main independent media in Bosnia and Herzegovina were the daily *Vecenje novine* (Sarajevo), the newspapers *Oslobodenje* (Sarajevo), *B-H Dani* (Sarajevo), *Blic* and *Slobodna Bosna* (Zenica) and the radios Studio 99 and Radio Zid (both from Sarajevo).

Radio or television programmes from abroad could be received in Sarajevo, but the problem was the electricity supply required to run a radio or television. In addition, only intellectuals understood foreign languages. Broadcasting in Serbo-Croat by the BBC, Deutsche Welle, Voice of America and Radio France International could be received almost everywhere in the former Yugoslavia.

The Federal Republic of Yugoslavia

The basic political and professional background in the Federal Republic of Yugoslavia (Serbia and Montenegro) was the same as in Bosnia and Herzegovina or Croatia, but working conditions for the media were perhaps even worse due to the United Nations embargo. The first thing Mr Milošević did in Serbia was to take control of all the important media, especially the electronic media. Radiotelevizija Srbije was fully state-owned and its editorial policy dictated by the government. The daily circulation of all the newspapers together was 300 000, whereas before the war several newspapers each had a wider circulation. In Serbia there were still truly independent media, such as *Vreme, Naša, Borba*, Radio B92 or Studio B. However, these were concentrated in Belgrade and had a very limited influence. This explains why they were tolerated by the regime, which could thus claim to be allowing a free press.

According to a journalist from Belgrade, working conditions were catastrophic. In mid-October *Vreme* had only enough paper for another four issues; afterwards it would be forced to stop. The newspaper had been living on donations, sponsorship (but advertising revenue was minimal) and solidarity. The only practical consequence of the announcement by the European Union of financial help was the accusation by the regime that *Vreme* was a foreign agent and therefore an enemy.

Some recent events led journalists to fear that the situation of independent media in Serbia would worsen. The government increased its propaganda against "traitors and fifth columnists"; more than 1 000 radio and television employees were placed on forced leave; an amendment was examined in parliament that would prevent the media from receiving help. Harassment and intimidation of journalists increased: Mr Dušan Relji, a journalist from *Vreme,* was kidnapped and interrogated for thirty-six hours by people who knew everything he had said, either publicly or privately, in the past four or five years; he was released through international pressure. The secret services also followed other journalists' activities. This situation led to the creation a journalists' solidarity fund, which organised several actions and took part in a campaign to supply food to journalists in Sarajevo with the help of the International Federation of Journalists.

In Kosovo, in 1989, when Yugoslavia started falling apart, the parliament was suppressed, the Albanian television in Priština was shut down and so was the daily newspaper *Rilindja*, although the population of Kosovo (2.3 million inhabitants) is 90% Albanian (the others being Serbs, Turks, Montenegrins, Roma/Gypsies, and so on).

In Vojvodina, all media were controlled. There were no genuinely independent media, despite various attempts. International sanctions did not appear to have an impact on the authorities.

In Montenegro there was clear evidence of state control. Seventy journalists lost their jobs, mainly from state-controlled media. A total media blackout on the radio, television and press took place. The President of the Association of Journalists and another journalist were sentenced to jail for offending the personality and functions of the President of Montenegro. Two Croat journalists and a journalist married to a Croat were sacked. There was an upsurge of hate-speech in the media. The rules on defamation were such that any critical comment could be stifled by the authorities. Some independent media survived such as the weekly *Monitor*, Radio Letinje and Radio Antenna M.

"The former Yugoslav Republic of Macedonia"

"The former Yugoslav Republic of Macedonia" was not really among those responsible for the disintegration of Yugoslavia. As nationalists did not win the elections nor, as a result, the battle for the media, the situation was not comparable to that of the other republics. There is a large range of opinions represented in the printed press, more than 100 private radio stations and some fifteen small local independent television stations, of which only A1 has a viewing public equivalent to that of the state television. Some of the newspaper and television and radio programmes are in Albanian, Turkish and other minority languages.

Unlike the other republics, "the former Yugoslav Republic of Macedonia" became independent without a single shot being fired. Its elections have been free and fair and the government has included Albanian ministers. The constitution guarantees the freedom of the press. A privatisation agency was set up in October 1993, but its programme did not include the media. The market was small and economic conditions rather difficult. The problem was to find a way in which the state would support the media without interfering with them.

According to the General Manager of the Macedonian Information Centre, the overall situation in the media field is quite relaxed and evolving, if slowly, in the right direction. The media need outside support, but of a different nature from that in Bosnia and Herzegovina, Croatia and Serbia. One of the main concerns of the profession is organisation: how to organise independent trade unions for journalists, how to organise independent media and how to organise a working relationship with the various institutions in place. Opposition papers carry open debates in the letters' pages. The tradition of tolerance in a multi-ethnic society and the existence of a critical, independent press, open to different currents of opinion, is enough to prevent the escalation of ethnic tensions.

Other sources, however, report government pressure particularly in broadcasting. The main problem would appear to have been economic, in so far as *Nova Makedonija* had a monopoly over printing, and to print elsewhere was costly. There were some fears that privatisation could lead to "sell-offs" of shares to "friends" of the government.

Action by professional and other non-governmental organisations

In February 1992 the Democratic Forum in Rijeka and the European Federation of Community Radios (FERL) organised a European colloquy on the freedom of the media in Rijeka-Fiume, Croatia. The Parliamentary Assembly was represented by Mrs Grendelmeier, Chairperson of the Sub-Committee on Media. The colloquy concluded that although European interventions would not provide the solution to the Yugoslav crisis they were, however, indispensable for creating the necessary conditions in which solutions could be developed by the local populations themselves.

In October 1992, during another colloquy organised by the FERL, thirty journalists from different republics of the former Yugoslavia, who refused the nationalist propaganda of the official media, decided to establish an independent information network, *Alternativna Informacija Mreža* (AIM). The network functions on a computer-based mailbox system covering the whole of the former Yugoslavia. Its aims were: to exchange articles and information between the republics of the former Yugoslavia, to prepare the ground for the creation of independent media and to provide an information service for media, institutions and NGOs outside the former Yugoslavia. From January 1993, the AIM network produced "Bura", a monthly, hour-long radio programme in Serbo-Croat, broadcast by independent radio stations within the former Yugoslavia and also for emigrant and refugee communities in Europe. It was made up of news, comments, interviews and specific dossiers.

Open Society Funds (Soros Foundations) were set up in all the countries of the former Yugoslavia, as well as in other central and eastern European countries and in the countries of the former Soviet Union. They were active in supporting independent media through donations of paper and equipment and the provision of technical assistance. In Croatia the Open Society Fund tried to help set up two independent radio stations, and in Belgrade it helped set up the Anti-War Media Centre.

For the first time ever the International Federation of Journalists and the International Federation of Newspaper Publishers joined efforts to face the dramatic situation of the media in the former Yugoslavia. They organised a round table on "Nationalism: a Crisis for Independent Journalism?", co-sponsored by Unesco and the Council of Europe (Ljubljana, February 1993). A resolution was then adopted, establishing a co-ordinating centre for independent media, open to independent journalists, publishers and broadcasters in the countries of the Balkan region, including the territories of the former Yugoslavia. The co-ordinating centre was set up in Ljubljana with financial assistance from Unesco, the Council of Europe, the Slovene Society of Journalists and the Open Society Fund (Slovenia), and began operating in April 1993.

In March of the same year the International Federation of Journalists and the International Federation of Newspaper Publishers sent a joint mission to Croatia to examine the situation of independent media, following which they made recommendations to the Government of Croatia and to the Council of Europe.

On 18 and 19 November 1993 a second round table was organised in Ljubljana by the International Federation of Journalists and the International Federation of Newspaper Publishers and funded by the Council of Europe entitled "Independent Media: A Key To Peace". The meeting found that the situation had deteriorated between February and November 1993. Thirty-nine journalists had been killed since the beginning of the conflict and at least another twenty were missing. Independent media and journalists that continued to survive and tried to report objectively were the victims of violence, harassment and economic and political asphyxiation. The meeting called, *inter alia*, for higher priority to be given to media initiatives, for the Ljubljana Co-ordinating Centre to be strengthened, for an examination of the effects of United Nations sanctions on independent media and for the facilitation of the movement of journalists.

Reporters sans frontières is a French-based non-governmental organisation concerned with the defence of press freedom and imprisoned journalists. In the former Yugoslavia the organisation was active in four complementary fields: investigating the situation of the press and journalists' working conditions; protesting against attacks on press freedom; conducting international press campaigns and supporting independent media. Concrete action in Bosnia and Herzegovina, Croatia, in "the former Yugoslav Republic of Macedonia" and Serbia was decided according to the following criteria: the importance of the medium (professional quality, degree of independence and influence on public opinion); the urgency of the situation and feasibility (cost, technical problems and security conditions).

Action by international organisations

Unesco supported the establishment of the Co-ordinating Centre for Independent Media in Ljubljana from the outset by providing the co-ordinator's salary for one year. It also launched training programmes for independent journalists and ran a special fund for assistance to independent media in the former Yugoslavia.

An *ad hoc* delegation of the European Parliament travelled to Croatia and Bosnia and Herzegovina in May 1993. It confirmed the strong feeling of abandonment in Sarajevo and proposed some concrete measures of support for the newspaper *Oslobodenje*.

The European Community Humanitarian Fund gave between 5 and 6 million ecus to the French organisation *Droit de parole* for running the radio boat, *Broda*, and for the support of four independent newspapers: *Oslobodenje* (Bosnia and Herzegovina), *Monitor* (Montenegro), *Vreme* and *Borba* as well as Radio B92 (Serbia). The European Community human rights budget, though only in principle able to supply small amounts, exceptionally granted 100 000 ecus to the AIM network.

The European Union has no specific budget line for supporting democratic forces and independent media in the former Yugoslavia except in Slovenia, which is eligible for Phare-Democracy programme support. Several approaches have been made to the commissioner responsible both from within the European Commission and from the European Parliament, but he has persistently vetoed any extension to the rest of the former Yugoslavia. One reason given is that the European Parliament vetoed Croatia's receiving funds from the Phare programme; another is the existing embargo against Serbia.

In March 1993 the Secretary General of the Council of Europe convened an informal meeting on the co-ordination of actions concerning the media in the former Yugoslavia. This meeting was attended by Mr Mazowiecki, Special Rapporteur of the United Nations Commission of Human Rights, and representatives of international and non-governmental organisations active in the field. Based on the conclusions of this meeting, the Secretary General proposed a double package of Council of Europe measures, which was accepted by the Committee of Ministers. This package included support for the Co-ordination Centre in Ljubljana and initiatives in the area of training of media professionals and was developed in co-operation with the International Federation of Journalists, the International Federation of Newspapers Publishers and the European Federation of Community Radios.

Following the joint mission of the International Federation of Journalists and the International Federation of Newspaper Publishers to Croatia and at the request of the Croatian Government, a mission of experts was organised by the Council of Europe in May 1993 to consider the legislative, regulatory and administrative framework for the media in Croatia. The team of experts formulated a number of critical remarks about that framework and made recommendations to the Croatian authorities. This was followed by a second Council of Europe mission in October 1993 to provide further assistance in the drafting of legislation on telecommunications and mail, and notably, the provisions dealing with private radio and television broadcasting.

In September 1993 Mrs Leni Fischer, Chair of the Committee on Culture and Education, addressed a written question to the Committee of Ministers on the situation of the media in the former Yugoslavia in which she called for rapid and effective support for independent media. In its reply the Committee of Ministers agreed on the importance of supporting independent media with a view to contributing to the peace process in the former Yugoslavia. However, the package of measures was largely implemented through voluntary contributions by governments and depended, therefore, very much on the latter's generosity

The situation of media in the former Yugoslavia varied from one country to another. Problems were much more acute in Serbia, Croatia and especially in Bosnia and Herzegovina than, for instance, in "the former Yugoslav Republic of Macedonia" or in Slovenia. However, while efforts should be concentrated on supporting the independent media in the first three countries, this should not mean that the others are forgotten.

It is clear that NGOs and intergovernmental organisations have played different roles. Whereas the former were more quickly able to help the independent media to survive by responding to their immediate material needs, the latter are in a better position to deal with long term problems more directly linked to the causes of the conflicts. This should not, however, prevent intergovernmental organisations from short-term action, in co-ordination with NGOs.

Media liberty at stake – the case of Croatia

The Public Information Act was adopted in 1992. In accordance with its provisions, a council of the protection of the freedom of the mass media was established in January 1995. However, the 1992 act was declared invalid by the Constitutional Court in late 1995.

There was much international criticism of the state-run Croatian television (HTV) which had a monopoly on nationwide broadcasts. The law on telecommunications was adopted in July 1994, but it appears that the advice of Council of Europe experts on certain essential points was not taken into account. Tenders were invited for establishing new radio and television stations both at national and at local levels. Due to numerous complaints, one round of invitations had to be repeated. Questions remained as to the fair distribution of frequencies. A number of (illegal) radio and tele-vision stations with pro-government tendencies were tolerated, while independent stations were ordered to stop broadcasting.

According to a report prepared by the Co-ordinating Centre for Independent Media of the Balkan Region, the International Federation of Journalists and the International Federation of News-paper Publishers in 1995, there were over 1 100 newspapers and magazines on the Croatian market. They were considered relatively free. However, few were considered independent of the influence of the government or the ruling party. Moreover, complaints were received from the Alternative Information Network (AIM) which was accused by President Tudjman of being "yugo-nostalgic" and therefore "an enemy of the people".

The Croatian authorities took measures against the media which were in clear contradiction of the commitments entered into under the Dayton Agreements. The offices of the weekly *Panorama*, which had repeatedly criticised the government, were closed for reasons of health and hygiene. A few days later charges were brought against journalists of the satirical weekly *Feral Tribune*, following an article criticising President Tudjman's plans to change a monument for victims of fascism in the Jasenovac camp into a monument for all victims of the second world war. It should be recalled that the government had already on previous occasions tried to put pressure on the *Feral Tribune* by imposing a so-called pornography tax. This measure, which was at the time severely criticised by the Assembly's rapporteurs, was subsequently annulled by the Croatian courts.

Electronic media: the status of Croatian Radio and Television (HRT)

Croatian Radio and Television (HRT) was set up by a special act of 1990 as a state-owned public enterprise with three TV and three radio channels. It was required to inform the public in a truthful, objective and prompt manner without representing the viewpoint of individual political parties, while respecting the principles of ethics, pluralism, tolerance, privacy and other freedoms and personal rights.

The HRT had its own supervisory council, the Radio-Television Council, consisting of thirty-five members (fifteen nominated by the parliament proportionally to its party structure, ten from various cultural institutions and religious communities and ten from the programming units). Moreover, the HRT had an administrative council, a director (appointed by the parliament), assisted by heads of departments (appointed by the government), and chief editors (appointed by the Radio-Television Council). The bylaws of HRT were issued by the administrative council in agreement with the government and the Radio-Television Council and the programming orientation was determined by the Radio-Television Council.

The HRT, being the most influential audiovisual medium with little competition from other broadcasting stations, was sufficiently independent from the state, having regard to the manner of appointment of its various organs. Moreover, some independent experts of the Council of Europe, when considering the (then draft) legislation on telecommunications, stressed the need to amend the most relevant provisions of the Act on Radio and Television, concerning the composition, mode of appointment of the director general and directors of HRT. No such amendments were made.

State secrets and defamation

On 29 March 1996, the Law on Modifications and Amendments of the Criminal Code of the Republic of Croatia was adopted by the Croatian Parliament. It was subsequently published in the official gazette *Narodne Novine* No. 28/96 of 12 April 1996, and came into effect from 20 April 1996. These modifications and amendments concerned the offence of defamation of high state officials (the President of the Republic of Croatia, the Speaker of the Croatian Parliament, the Presidents of the Supreme and the Constitutional Court of Croatia) and the revealing of state or military secrets.

As to the former, the amendments related to the manner in which criminal proceedings were initiated. Up until then, proceedings had been initiated by the Public Prosecutor upon a proposal by the state official. According to the amendments, the state official concerned does not need to request prosecution, but only give his or her written consent for legal action undertaken by the Public Prosecutor. The initiative and responsibility now lies mainly with the latter. It would be much easier for a high state official to give consent for action already undertaken by the Public Prosecutor than to initiate proceedings him or herself. It is indicative that until now not a single action has been undertaken by high state officials on defamation. Public addresses made by high state officials show that they wish, on the basis of the amendments, to impose discipline upon the media by threatening them with criminal prosecution. Thus, the amendments were not legally essential, but may have stimulated self-censorship and further limited freedom of expression.

Regarding the amendments concerning the revelation of state or military secrets, a new provision was added to the Criminal Code, according to which a person who publishes the contents (entirely or partly) of a document or data known to be a state or military secret may be prosecuted and punished by fine or imprisonment for up to three years.[1] A state or military secret is defined as a document or data which has, or could have, damaging consequences for the political, military and economic interests of the country. The very fact that publication of a state or military secret is made a criminal act is not problematic in itself. What gave reason for concern was that no clear criteria were defined on what was secret, so that an unlimited list of information could be considered secret, while the mere risk that the information could have damaging consequences sufficed for prosecution. Moreover, it is very doubtful that such far-reaching limitations of the freedom of expression for the protection of "political, economic and military interests of the state" are compatible with the stipulation of the Croatian Constitution which permits such restrictions only for the protection of the "legal order", and even more so with he stipulations of Article 10 of the European Convention on Human Rights. In fact, according to the Co-ordinating Centre for Independent

---

1. Up until now a criminal act could have been committed only by a person who was in possession of a state or military secret (due to his profession or position) and who conveyed it to another person without authorisation.

Media of the Balkan Region the above-mentioned amendments were not only contrary to the European Convention on Human Rights but also to the Croatian Constitution.

The recent amendments to the Criminal Code should be reconsidered by the Croatian authorities as they reinforce the impression that freedom of the media is not sufficiently guaranteed in Croatia. The Constitutional Court could, of course, be seized in order to decide upon their constitutionality, while every ordinary court in Croatia could interpret and apply the new provisions in a restrictive manner offering to some extent the missing definitions and criteria.

Finally, another event of serious concern in the field of the media is related to the obligation imposed on *Novi List*, a leading independent newspaper, to pay backdated customs, duties and taxes amounting to 3.5 million Deutschmarks.

The situation with regard to the exercise of freedom of the press in Croatia was particularly worrying.

It appears to have been one of the most fundamental human rights problems persisting in Croatia. Serious allegations of intimidation and suspected manipulations by state authorities as well as extensive state control over the electronic media have been made. As democracy cannot flourish without free and independent media, the Croatian Government has to take active steps to secure compliance with the principles of Article 10 of the European Convention on Human Rights.

Reconstruction

Aid for reconstruction

Reconstruction: a peace-time challenge

Progress on reconstruction has had a direct effect on the return of refugees and displaced persons – factors such as housing, the state of infrastructure, the availability of medical treatment and the education system have been crucial. There are other less direct but no less important relationships – economic recovery is essential to reduce the alarming unemployment rate (90% in some regions), which is worsening as demobilisation continues apace.

The reconstruction process was successfully launched. The donors met in Brussels on 12 and 13 April 1996 and pledged investments of some US$ 1.8 thousand million. A series of practical projects had already been devised and at least part of the funding had been found for them. The donors co-ordinate their activities by means of task forces for the various areas of reconstruction which meet regularly in Sarajevo. However, this process is too slow and the funds pledged insufficient.

Disregarding the humanitarian aid and funds provided by various international authorities, very few funds have been used on the ground. The huge gap between the preparation of projects and their implementation has been mentioned on numerous occasions by Bosnian representatives. Therefore, the reconstruction process has had to be speeded up considerably. The people of Bosnia and Herzegovina will have to draw the dividends of peace in order to believe that it will last. In the view of the people we spoke to, one US dollar spent in 1996 was worth ten spent the following year.

Put in stark but realistic terms, if no economic results of the peace are forthcoming, then that peace has little chance of surviving. Nationwide unemployment is estimated at over 70%, and it reaches 80% in Sarajevo and 90% in certain areas, such as Gorazde. Industrial production stands at only 10% of its pre-war level.

Given the magnitude of the reconstruction task, the question becomes: what should come first: "micro" or "macro" assistance? The uncomfortable answer is both.

At "micro" level it has become urgent to embark on ambitious housing reconstruction in order to shelter the people. Rebuilding of existing, but damaged buildings and construction of new homes are also needed to encourage refugees and displaced people to return, including those who cannot return to their region of origin. The Office of the United Nations High Commissioner for Refugees, recognising the strong ethnic division of the country at this moment, has concentrated its reconstruction efforts on about a dozen priority areas to which refugees are more likely to return.

The scale of the problems is frightening. Tuzla, for example, has seen its population increase from 100 000 to 160 000 people, with 30% of its buildings destroyed.

The Dayton Agreements foresaw the establishment of a Commission for Real Property Claims of Displaced Persons and Refugees. People who lost their property after April 1992 can make a claim to the commission for the return of that property, for an exchange of property, or for compensation. Between 600 000 and 2 million claims are expected in due course. Apart from the sheer magnitude of the task, the commission will be faced with numerous difficulties, such as trying to trace lost property records, making people aware of its existence and ensuring co-operation from the different parts of the country. It is also unclear who will eventually foot the bill for the presumably huge compensation sums involved. Nevertheless, the commission is an essential tool for bringing back to Bosnia and Herzegovina a semblance of order so necessary for economic reconstruction. Its work is very sensitive and needs the political guidance of the international community in order to prevent a worsening of the already pronounced ethnic divisions.

Assistance at "macro" level has been as important as that at micro level in restarting the economy : generation and transmission of electricity, water supplies, communications and transport and the repair of roads. Restoring these sectors will be necessary to help industry and small businesses resume their activities.

In a country where planning for reconstruction is almost totally absent due to the ravages of war and the limited authority of the Sarajevo Government, the World Bank fulfils a critical function. Its objective in Bosnia and Herzegovina is to support a broad-based rehabilitation of infrastructure and the social sectors capable of jump-starting economic recovery, growth and jobs ; to strengthen and rebuild institutions ; and to support, in parallel, the transition to a market-based economy. Its resources will be used as "seed capital" to co-finance projects across a broad range of sectors in co-operation with of a variety of donors, including the Council of Europe's Social Development Fund. The Fund must be encouraged to make greater efforts in providing housing for displaced persons and minorities, including Roma/Gypsies.

The loans given by the World Bank to Bosnia and Herzegovina are very favourable. They are generally to be paid back within thirty-five years, include a ten-year grace period and carry 0% interest. The Bank does not finance projects alone, but contributes 25% of the necessary funds, with the international donor community, especially the European Union, supplying the rest. There is close co-operation with the European Union on various projects, and also contacts with the Social Development Fund of the Council of Europe. The European Commission contributes considerable resources, notably through its Phare Essential Aid Programme.

The World Bank plans its projects on the basis of the work of about a dozen different task forces. In December 1995 it pledged US$ 150 million which was earmarked for a first group of seven emergency projects financed from a special trust fund drawn from the Bank's yearly profits. The emergency projects include: an emergency recovery project; farm reconstruction; water, sanitation and solid waste; transport reconstruction; rehabilitation of war victims; education and district heating. In June 1996 all seven projects were approved by the World Bank and a limited disbursement of funds began.

Thirteen additional projects, financed through the International Development Agency (IDA), have involved electric power, land mine clearance, public works and employment, local initiatives, demobilisation support and reintegration, gas rehabilitation, housing reconstruction, hospital services, education, transport, forestry, water management and a transition assistance credit.

The World Bank's action should be seen within the context of the donor pledges made by the international community in two successive conferences in Brussels, totalling nearly US$ 1.3 thousand million. This is, however, only a small part of the US$ 5.4 thousand million estimated by the World Bank as necessary for reconstruction in the first three post-war years. The Bosnian and Herzegovian Government for its part told the Parliamentary Assembly delegation that the country needs US$ 80 thousand million for reconstruction!

The World Bank is acutely aware that reaching this sum of US$ 5.4 thousand million – or even disbursing the US$ 1.3 thousand million

– will, to borrow the words of the Assembly's Recommendation 1297 (1996), "depend on the clear prospect of stability and the goodwill of all the former parties to the conflict".

The World Bank was placed in something of a dilemma. On the one hand it wished to go ahead with the projects, and actually brought down the time required from conception to approval of a given proposal from some ten months to only two. On the other hand it felt it had to "hurry slowly" in order to ensure the diligent use of resources. It therefore paid for the projects little by little. This was not, of course, to the full liking of the Bosnian and Herzegovian Government in Sarajevo.

All in all, however, the World Bank policy seems a reasonable compromise between the urgency of assistance and the need to ensure the best use of scarce resources on behalf of the donor community, but above all on behalf of Bosnia and Herzegovina itself, which will ultimately have to repay the loans. At any rate, of the twenty most immediate projects in the World Bank's Priority Reconstruction Programme in Bosnia and Herzegovina, seven projects totalling US$ 553 million were approved by the Bank in June 1996, while another thirteen, totalling US$ 931 million were approved by the end of that year. The economic stimulus provided by all these projects began to be felt in the country.

With regard to the co-ordination of all the international efforts to help Bosnia and Herzegovina economically, the World Bank said that its task forces were functioning better each day and served as a kind of planning nucleus for the international donor community. However, it said, this did not prevent a certain degree of confusion from occurring at different stages of the assistance process.

For one thing, the host country authorities, both at national and local level, often negotiate with several donors at the same time, hoping that if one refuses, another will go along. Furthermore, as the Assembly delegation discovered, the Sarajevo Government has little or no say over what happens in, say, Tuzla (not to mention the Republika Srpska, or even Herzegovina), rendering nationwide infrastructure investments difficult to implement. All this can create frustration among donors.

Another source of confusion is reported to come from the varied nature of aid sources. Some aid is multilateral (such as through the World Bank, the European Union and the Social Development Fund), whereas other aid is bilateral, that is to say from one donor country, or comes through non-governmental organisations. In certain recipient countries this would not have posed so much of a problem, but in a Bosnia and Herzegovina lacking in finances, staff and even physical facilities, the absorption capacity to channel aid usefully is quickly reached.

Another difficulty, previously hinted at, lies in the hesitation on the part of private investors and official donors alike as regards the future political stability of the country, or indeed its future existence. The World Bank, to allay such fears, approved a special political risk guarantee facility to protect lenders against losses arising from war, civil disturbance or political interference. However, such a guarantee will, needless to say, raise the cost of financing and may not be sufficient to attract certain potential investors.

If, on the one hand, the people of Bosnia and Herzegovina need to see rapid economic progress in order to start believing in the peace process, then it is also true that official international assistance must be supplemented by private investment if any sustained development is to be expected.

Here the responsibility rests mainly with the host country. In essence, investment will start flowing only if true political stability can be achieved. It is not enough just to hold elections, these also have to be seen as free, fair and extending to the country's whole territory.

Sustainable economic development will also need effective political authority over the whole country and a firm legal framework within which business can operate. There will have to be general confidence on the part of investors as regards the country's future. If this is true for the Sarajevo area, then it is even more valid for two regions also visited by the Assembly delegation: Gorazde, about 100 kilometres south-east of the capital; and Tuzla, about 200 kilometres to the north-east.

In 1996 Gorazde's situation was especially precarious. It could only be reached by crossing over the territory of the Republika Sprska in convoys of limited size escorted by Multinational Implementation Force troops three times a week. Gorazde lacked virtually everything: wood and fuel for heating, electricity and even telecommunications. The World Bank prepared the financing of a road across the mountains, within Bosnian territory, for about US$ 60 million, planned for 1999 at the earliest. Meanwhile, no co-operation whatsoever was proffered by the surrounding authorities of the Republika Sprska. Gorazde therefore had to rely on support from Sarajevo and abroad for some considerable time. One priority task will be simply to clean up the heaps of rubbish littering the banks of the town's waterways, not least to avoid the risk of outbreaks of epidemic.

The situation in Tuzla is less precarious but still preoccupying. Tuzla used to be among the wealthier regions in the former Yugoslavia, with a strong industrial base including an advanced chemical industry. Today it is largely paralysed, with an 80% unemployment rate, but unlike Gorazde it is not cut off from the rest of the country. What Tuzla needs above all is a link to the north connecting it with the rest of Europe. The city would seem an ideal recipient of funds from the Council of Europe's Social Development Fund, in particular as concerns housing and rubbish collection.

Generally speaking, Bosnia and Herzegovina desperately needs to improve its trade relations with Europe and with the rest of the Balkan region in particular. Trade between Bosnia and Herzegovina and the Republika Sprska to the east is virtually non-existent, while that with Croatia appears limited.

The foreign debt burden is a considerable obstacle to economic development in the eyes of the government in Sarajevo. It maintains that 25% of all the aid it receives has to be used immediately to service the foreign debt. Furthermore, no agreement to reduce or reschedule the US$ 3 thousand million in foreign debt has been reached with the international financial community, such as the London Club.

The question of whether the international community is supplying sufficient aid to Bosnia and Herzegovina has been raised. On the one hand, the country's economic situation must improve quickly and be seen by the people to do so. On the other hand, much of the assistance given may be wasted unless there is a host government capable of channelling the money and making sure that it can lead to a revival of the economy at regional and local level, rather than allowing it to fall on barren ground.

There is the further question of whether co-ordination of assistance needs to be improved. This is surely the case, but who should do it: the international community or the host country? Surely the answer must be that this is primarily the responsibility of the latter, but, as we have seen, the Sarajevo Government as well as regional and local authorities are seriously overstretched, and there are few links between them. Indeed, the most convincing overall reconstruction concept the delegation saw was the one provided by the World Bank, working intimately with the High Representative, the

European Union and others. Some of the international donor institutions we spoke to also complained that local politics frequently interferes with the planning of projects.

Council of Europe Social Development Fund

The primary purpose of the Fund – to help European countries in resolving the social problems resulting from the presence of refugees and displaced persons – makes it a specialised instrument for intervention in war-stricken regions.

Approval was given by the Fund bodies, on 22 April 1996, to a project granting Bosnia and Herzegovina US$ 5 million in order to finance a rehabilitation programme for war victims and refugees. Special procedures, in addition to great imagination and professionalism, were required in order for the loan to be granted. A second loan, amounting to US$ 1.5 million, allocated for the reconstruction of Tuzla's drinking water supply system, was approved on 20 January 1997, but has yet to be paid.

However, apart from these commendable efforts, it should be observed that member states, in particular large states, are reluctant to participate in the projects for Bosnia and Herzegovina, and to provide guarantees and assist with funding. Since Bosnia and Herzegovina is not a member of the Fund, other states are obliged to submit and guarantee the projects which concern it.

Furthermore, the preparation of serious projects requires, in particular under the conditions prevailing in Bosnia and Herzegovina, the presence of experts in the country, at least on a temporary basis. The World Bank, European Community and so on are operating on this basis. No one will provide ready made projects free of charge complete with funding. Consequently, the Fund bodies are urged to consider the best way in which to enhance its participation in the preparation of projects in Bosnia and Herzegovina.

Implementing the Dayton Agreements

The Dayton Agreements constitute a comprehensive approach to a peace settlement. They deal with military aspects, security, reconstruction, human rights, democracy, the rule of law, refugees and arms control. The responsibility for implementation is shared by a large number of international organisations.

The Erdut Agreement

The Agreement on the Peaceful Reintegration of Eastern Slavonia, Baranja and Western Sirmium, concluded between the Croatian Government and Serbian representatives on 12 November 1995 at Erdut, established a framework for the gradual transfer of control over the region to the Croatian Government. A transitional United Nations administration (Untaes) was put in place for a period of twelve months, with a possible extension of a further twelve months. At the end of this period, the region was completely reintegrated into Croatia.

Unlike the Dayton Agreements, the Erdut Agreement is extremely detailed, foreseeing strict adherence to various stages. Implementation is essentially on track and has already resulted in demilitarisation, the opening of certain roads, the partial resumption of trade in goods, and the re-establishment of a number of communication facilities.

Eastern Slavonia, that is, the easternmost region of Croatia north of Bosnia and Herzegovina and bordering on the Yugoslav Federation used to be a very prosperous region, rich in oil, agriculture and industry.

The territory in question includes between 130 000 and 150 000 inhabitants, the vast majority of whom are of Serbian ethnic origin. About 10% of them are of Croatian ethnic origin. In addition to the original population, there are Serbian refugees from Western Slavonia and Krajina who came to the region following the Croatian army offensives in 1995; their numbers are estimated at several tens of thousands. Many dwellings were destroyed during the war, in particular in Vukovar, a town which was martyred in 1991. About 60% of the population is unemployed, and their numbers are increasing with the progressive demobilisation under way.

The first stages of the implementation of the Erdut Agreement went ahead as scheduled. Working parties in different sectors bringing together Croatian authorities and Serbian representatives were set up, demilitarisation went well, the Zagreb-Belgrade motorway was opened, the postal service re-established and Croatian customs officials deployed at the border between Eastern Slavonia and Serbia proper.

Crucial stages still had to be completed – the return of displaced persons, economic reconstruction, human rights guarantees and the introduction of democratically elected local authorities: ensuring the return of displaced persons of Croatian origin, reassuring the Serbian population in the region and providing prospects of a normal life for all concerned.

As far as the return of displaced persons is concerned, in the same way as in Bosnia and Herzegovina two decisive aspects came into play: physical and material security. With regard to the first of the two, the Croatian Parliament adopted a law on amnesty which was undoubtedly a step in the right direction.

However, the representatives of international organisations, as well as those from Serbia, have emphasised that if the text is to have the results intended, it should have been more explicit and its scope broadened in order to apply to everyone, with the exception of those who have committed war crimes.

With regard to material security, houses needed to be repaired and built urgently and, in general terms, the local economy needed to be put back on its feet. It should be emphasised that prior to the conflict, Slavonia was one of the richest regions in the former Yugoslavia.

About fifteen projects have been prepared and forwarded to potential donors. Thus far, certain promises of funding have been made; however, successful reconstruction requires greater funding at a more rapid pace.

Similarly, for confidence to be restored, the increased presence of international and NGO observers proved necessary. The arrival of the Joint Committee on Police, made up of 150 Croat police officers of Serbian nationality and 150 Croats, trained abroad, was eagerly awaited.

Even if the situation in Eastern Slavonia seemed less complex than that in Bosnia and Herzegovina, the challenges were similar and also quite considerable. It became vital to guarantee the freedom of the media and the emergence of a pluralist political system; these are essential conditions if leaders are to be elected to work in the interests of citizens. In fact, just as in Bosnia and Herzegovina, the normalisation process is often delayed by virtue of the fact that the people who are in power have a personal interest in main-taining instability and the absence of the rule of law.

It was also necessary that progress towards peace not be hampered by unrealistic requests from certain Serbian representatives aiming to achieve autonomy, which included having their own currency and different passports.

It is still too early to talk about any economic development in Eastern Slavonia. Unemployment stands at 60%, in a population which has swollen to some 150 000 people (half of them displaced).

The United Nations administration has performed admirable work under very difficult conditions, but it needed greater material support from the international community. Its priorities were the rebuilding of essential infrastructure, job creation, housing and building up of an interim administration until the region could be fully reintegrated into Croatia.

Principles of the Dayton Agreements

The agreements, initialled in Dayton (Ohio) on 21 November 1995, are a remarkable achievement of United States diplomacy. They represent a transformation of policy from "peace-keeping" to "peace-enforcement". This transformation was made possible by the pressures exerted by the economic boycott and by a United States decision to commit troops on the ground in Bosnia and Herzegovina. On 18 December 1995, Unprofor transferred authority to a 60 000-strong Nato-led Multinational Implementation Force, with a 20 000-strong United States contingent. It was the outcome of a chain of events which began in mid-August 1995 with President Clinton's veto on a move by the United States Congress to end the arms embargo.

The Dayton Agreements are built up from the elements of a whole series of prior agreements – including the Vance-Owen and Owen-Stoltenberg peace plans. They encompass much of the content of the Washington Agreement of February 1994. They give substance to the Agreed Principles and Further Agreed Principles of New York and Geneva, September 1995.

Their aim, of course, is to end the war and enable Bosnia and Herzegovina to function as a single political unit. They consist of a short "general framework" and twelve annexes (numbered from 1A and 1B to 11). Their structure can more simply be seen in terms of a three-phase medical analogy:

- *stabilise the condition of the patient* (annexes 1A-1B-2-4-5): agreement on a "two-entity" constitution (the Federation of Bosnia and Herzegovina and the Republika Srpska) and an "inter-entity" boundary line, a commitment to arbitration of disputes between the entities, a ceasefire line and separation zone as a basis for moving to the inter-entity boundary line and separation zone (with consequent exchanges of territory), and a commitment to arms control and confidence-building measures;

- *prescribe remedies* (annexes 3-6-7-8-9): a provisional election commission (for elections within six to nine months), a commission for human rights, a commission for refugees and displaced persons, a commission for national monuments, a commission for public corporations (transport, communications, energy, water);

- *administer the treatment* (annexes 10-11): designation of a high representative to co-ordinate the activities of civilian organisations and agencies by means of a "joint civilian commission", to provide guidance to an international police task force (with advisory, monitoring and training functions), and to liaise with the Multinational Implementation Force commander through the "joint military commission".

Role of the Council of Europe and of other European organisations

The Dayton Agreements provide an unprecedented frame and opportunity for the concerted efforts of a wide array of international organisations, most of which have been present for some years "on the ground" in Bosnia and Herzegovina. These organisations range from Nato, the United Nations and its specialised agencies (notably the Office of the United Nations High Commissioner for Refugees), the OSCE (for arms control and the elections), the European Union (notably for economic reconstruction but also for continued "monitoring" in co-operation with the OSCE) and the International Committee of the Red Cross (exchange of prisoners).

The expertise of the Council of Europe in the field of human rights is recognised a number of times in the agreements:

– In Article II.2 of the constitution, it is provided that: "The rights and freedoms set forth in the European Convention for the Protection of Human Rights and Fundamental Freedoms shall apply directly (...) [and] (...) have priority over all other law."

– In the Human Rights Commission set up under the constitution, consisting of an ombudsperson and a chamber, it is provided that the Committee of Ministers of the Council of Europe should appoint eight members of the fourteen-member chamber and should designate its president. It is stipulated that none of the Council of Europe appointees should be citizens of Bosnia and Herzegovina or of neighbouring states. The six remaining members are designated by the entities themselves – four by the federation and two by the Republika Srpska. The ombudsperson, whose appointment is entrusted to the OSCE chairmanship, is former Permanent Representative to the Council of Europe of Switzerland (and former member of the Parliamentary Assembly) Gret Haller.

– The selection of three judges for the Constitutional Court and of three members (including the president) of the Commission for Displaced Persons and Refugees is entrusted to the President of the European Court of Human Rights.

Under similar dispositions, the appointment of a member of the five-member Commission for National Monuments (and the designation of its chairman) is entrusted to the Director-General of Unesco; and the appointment of two members of the five-member Commission on Public Corporations (and the designation of its chairman) is entrusted to the President of the European Bank for Reconstruction and Development (EBRD). If the two entities fail to agree on the name of a third arbitrator for disputed portions of the inter-entity boundary line, the appointment will be entrusted to the President of the International Court of Justice.

It is clear, too – not under the agreements but by virtue of Bosnia and Herzegovina's request for membership of our Organisation – that the Council of Europe has had a role to play in connection with the first elections. The task of certifying social and political conditions as suitable for effective elections fell to the OSCE. It was the Head of the OSCE Mission in Bosnia and Herzegovina who acted as chairman and made appointments to the Provisional Election Commission, which included the High Representative and representatives of the state and of each entity: "In the event of disputes within the Commission, the decision of the Chairman shall be final". Through its "assistance and co-operation" programmes – notably in the fields of civil society and the rule of law and the media – the Council of Europe has contributed to these conditions.

Organisation of the first democratic elections in Bosnia and Herzegovina (14 September 1996)

The Dayton Agreements, signed on 21 November 1995, entrusted the task of organising the elections in Bosnia and Herzegovina (BiH) to the OSCE. A mission and the Provisional Election Commission were set up in Sarajevo, both headed by United States Ambassador Robert H Frowick.

The Dayton Agreements stipulated that the OSCE must certify whether conditions existed for the effective holding of the elections. A set of criteria was prepared by the Provisional Electoral

Commission, on 1 February 1996. On 25 June 1996, the OSCE Chairman-in-Office, Swiss Foreign Minister Flavio Cotti, announced that, despite remaining difficulties, the elections would be held on 14 September 1996.

Organisation of the elections

On 28 June 1996 the Bureau of the Assembly established an *ad hoc* committee of observers for the elections in Bosnia and Herzegovina.

A former Dutch Minister of the Interior and former Mayor of Amsterdam Mr Ed van Thijn was appointed Co-ordinator of International Monitoring. He was to report directly to the OSCE Chairman-in-Office.

The election rules envisaged that voters would, in principle, vote where they were registered as residing in the census of 1991. This rule applied without exception to the voters who had not changed their residence since 1991. Refugees ("external" refugees, currently living abroad) and displaced persons ("internal" refugees, currently forced to live in parts of Bosnia and Herzegovina different from their place of residence in 1991) had three options:

– to go and vote in person in the municipality where they lived in 1991 (which, in many cases, involved crossing the inter-entity border line (IEBL));

– to use Form I to register to vote via absentee ballot in the municipalities where they lived prior to 1991;

– to use Form II to register to vote in person in a municipality other than that in which they resided at the time of the 1991 census, which could be where they currently resided (this was only valid for displaced persons) or where they intended to reside.

On 27 August 1996 the Chairman of the Provisional Election Commission, Ambassador Frowick, announced the decision to postpone the municipal elections, as the conditions resulting from the Dayton Agreement had been insufficiently respected at municipal level. There had been reports of pressure on voters to register, using the possibility of Form II, and to vote in municipalities other than those where they lived prior to 1991. This was clearly aimed at consolidating ethnic majorities in the areas that had been cleansed during the war.

The external (refugee) vote took place from 28 August to 3 September in fifty-five countries. The refugees could vote either by post or in person at designated polling stations. Some 641 000 voters registered to vote and the estimated overall turnout was about 63%.

After the postponement of municipal elections, six bodies remained to be elected:

Bosnia and Herzegovina

- The presidency of Bosnia and Herzegovina (3 members);
- The House of Representatives of the Parliament (28 members from the federation and 14 from the Republika Srpska);

Federation of Bosnia and Herzegovina

- The House of Representatives of the Parliament;
- The Cantonal Assemblies (10 cantons).

Republika Srpska

- The President and Vice President of the Republika Srpska;
- The National Assembly of the Republika Srpska.

The vote took place on 14 September at 4 400 ordinary and 200 absentee polling stations. It took place on the basis of the voters' list, which the Provisional Election Commission had asked the Bosnian Central Statistical Institute to produce by updating the

1991 census. Since its original publication the provisional voters list had been revised twice in order to make it more accurate. Voters had had a chance to check it and to inform the institute of any necessary correction to the data.

Observations on the elections

There were no significant incidents on election day. This was partly due to the massive and very visible presence of the Multinational Implementation Force and the International Police Task Force. The local police were primarily responsible for security. The reports available so far indicate that there were no serious complaints concerning their conduct on election day.

On the whole, the election procedures in the polling stations visited by the members of the *ad hoc* committee on election day were conducted properly, and the members of the voting stations committees were, in the majority of cases, competent and up to their tasks.

A number of irregularities were noted. However, given the extreme complexity of these elections (six different elections, absentee voting, and so on), the conduct of the election procedures on election day may be regarded as satisfactory. Among more serious irregularities one should mention aggressive behaviour of some party representatives who were occasionally even giving information or instructions to voters or members of the polling committee. There was an interruption in the counting of the ballots in Mrkonjić Grad in the Republika Srpska, ordered by Pale and Banja Luka. The reason for this incident was that the Local Election Committee (LEC) had not been informed of the way the voting of refugees and displaced persons had taken place. Its members expressed suspicion with regard to the number of ballots that were brought in from Sarajevo. They claimed that not all the names of the refugees that had already voted had been deleted from the voters' list.

If there were no serious objections to the manner in which the election procedures were respected at the polling stations, three problems of a more general nature were observed: the insufficient number of absentee polling stations and difficulties with the supply of proper ballot papers to these stations; the significant number of voters whose names were not on the voters' list, and the extremely low number of refugees and displaced persons that came in person to vote in the municipalities where they resided in 1991.

The number of polling stations intended for absentees was clearly insufficient and large crowds of people were observed at a number of them. In the region of Mostar the situation was further aggravated by the fact that there were not enough ballots for voters who intended to vote in some municipalities in the Republika Srpska. Fortunately, as the municipal elections had been postponed, the ballot papers for all the municipalities in the Republika Srpska were identical. The surplus ballot papers from some municipalities were thus used for voting in others, simply by changing the name on the envelope containing the ballot papers. In spite of this a number of people were denied the right to vote. It is our impression that this problem could have had much more serious consequences if the municipal elections had not been postponed. If they had been held, each absentee station would have had to have a sufficient number of different ballots for each municipality in Bosnia and Herzegovina. Thus, the risk of confusion and lack of ballot papers would have been even greater.

The fact that absentee voting was, in a majority of cases, only possible in the specially designated absentee stations may have intimidated some voters, in particular in the Republika Srpska where such voting was clearly discouraged.

The second major problem concerns missing names on the municipal voters' list. According to the preliminary statement of the Co-ordinator for International Monitoring, problems with voters identification were observed in 11% of the voting stations. This number seemed to be rather low, as our observers encountered this problem in virtually all the polling stations visited. It is true that percentages of people who were not found on the voters' lists varied, from only a few to some 5% to 10% of all voters who came to vote to a particular voting station. This raised suspicion, particularly in the Republika Srpska, where some speculated that most of the voters missing from the voters lists were Serbs. It is interesting that a number of these voters had checked their names on the provisional voters lists and that problems obviously occurred during the last revision of this list. The number of people who were actually denied the right to vote because of this was not negligible.

The third major problem concerns the number of refugees and displaced persons who voted in person in the municipalities where they resided prior to 1991. Their number was much lower than initially estimated. Apparently only some 15 000 people crossed the inter-entity border line, although initial estimates were 90 000 to 100 000. Added to this figure is the number of refugees who decided not to cross the international frontiers and the displaced persons who did not cross the inter-ethnic boundaries within the federation. For these voters, there were no alternatives to voting elsewhere or with an absentee ballot. The deadline to register for such voting had expired on 30 July. It should be noted that people crossing the inter-entity border line could only vote for the presidential candidates from the entity where they voted. For example, the voters crossing to the Republika Srpska could only vote for one of the Serb candidates and those crossing to vote in the federation could only choose between Croat and Bosnian candidates.

Some other elements of the entire electoral process, in particular the conduct of the election campaign and the freedom and independence of the media, were clearly below the Council of Europe standards for free and fair elections. The commitments concerning the right to campaign had been systematically ignored through intimidation, organised violence and disruption of opposition party meetings.

Freedom of expression and non-discriminatory access to the media were insufficient to create that conditions favourable to free and fair elections. Although the overall image remains bleak, there were some signs of improvement in the run up to the elections, thanks to the efforts of the international community and the courage and determination of some local Bosnian journalists. A particularly encouraging example was that of the local radio station in Konjić, where both the SDA and its opponents (Party for Bosnia and Herzegovina and the Social Democrats) expressed their satisfaction with its pre-election broadcasting and the access they had to its facilities.

First election statistics

Estimated current population: 3.5 million
(Bosnian-Croat Federation 2.5 million, Republika Srpska 1 million).

Ethnic composition of prewar population:
43.7% Bosnian, 31.3% Serb, 17.7% Croat.

Total number of registered voters: 2.9 million
(including 641 000 refugees registered in 55 countries).

Estimated number of voters who voted: 2.32 million
(1.3 million in the federation, 1.02 million in the Republika Srpska, these numbers include some 500 000 absentee votes)

The institutions for the protection of human rights in Bosnia and Herzegovina

Introduction

The Washington Agreements of February 1994, followed by the Dayton Agreements, signed on 14 December 1995, have given Bosnia and Herzegovina a particularly advanced body of instruments and machinery for protecting human rights.

The Council of Europe and its Parliamentary Assembly have made a significant contribution to this situation. In 1992, the Assembly adopted Recommendation 1183 on access by European non-member states to institutions operating under certain Council of Europe conventions relating to human rights, followed in 1993 by Recommendation 1204 on the creation of a transitional mechanism for the protection of human rights in European non-member states of the Council of Europe, and culminating in the Committee of Ministers' adoption of Resolution (93) 6 on the control of respect for human rights in European states not yet members of the Council of Europe. The latter contained the seeds of Appendix 6 of the Dayton Agreements.

The Dayton Agreements, signed on 14 December 1995 by the Republic of Bosnia and Herzegovina, the Republic of Croatia and the Federal Republic of Yugoslavia (on behalf of the Republika Srpska), recognised the State of Bosnia and Herzegovina (BiH), which is composed of two entities: the Federation of Bosnia and

Herzegovina (FBH) and the Republika Srpska (RS). Each of these has institutions to protect human rights, as well as civil institutions such as their own parliaments, governments, judicial systems and police. Article I of Annexe 4 of the Dayton Agreements, which concerns the Constitution of Bosnia and Herzegovina, and Annexe 6 are devoted to human rights. Appendix I of Annexe 4 lists the human rights agreements that will apply in Bosnia and Herzegovina.

The institutions of the State of Bosnia and Herzegovina

Article II of the Constitution of Bosnia and Herzegovina, which deals with human rights and fundamental freedoms, states that Bosnia and Herzegovina and the entities "shall ensure the highest level of internationally recognised human rights and fundamental freedoms". A Commission on Human Rights for Bosnia and Herzegovina has been set up as provided for in Annexe 6 of the Dayton Agreements.

The Commission on Human Rights

The commission comprises two bodies: the Office of the Ombudsperson and the Chamber of Human Rights.

The Ombudsperson for Human Rights

The OSCE appointed Mrs Gret Haller Ombudsperson for Human Rights for a period of five years. At the end of this period, the Ombudsperson will be appointed by the State President of Bosnia and Herzegovina. The institution of Ombudsperson is intended to be permanent, unlike the chamber, which will disappear once Bosnia and Herzegovina becomes a member of the Council of Europe and its citizens are granted access to the European Court of Human Rights.

At first sight, this two-level system appears to be based on the machinery of the European Convention on Human Rights. However, the Office of the Ombudsperson does not play exactly the same role as the European Commission of Human Rights or the Chamber that of the Court.[1]

In practice, applications can be made to the Ombudsperson, or to the Chamber directly if the applicants so wish (Article V.1 of Appendix 6 of the Dayton Agreements). The rules of procedure of the two institutions making up the Commission on Human Rights provide for the same conditions of admissibility, which are based on those of the European Convention on Human Rights: the exhaustion of domestic remedies, if these exist; and actions or decisions occurring after 15 December 1995, other than in cases where an earlier violation continues beyond that date.

The Ombudsperson's role is to mediate between the parties. If mediation is not possible, the Ombudsperson can either refer the case to the Chamber, or adopt a final report on the subject.

The major contrast with the machinery of the European Convention on Human Rights is that the Ombudsperson can take up cases on his or her own initiative and submit special reports, on specific issues, to any governmental authority. The latter must then reply within the period specified by the Ombudsperson.

The Office of the Ombudsperson was opened in Sarajevo in March 1996. In accordance with Article III, paragraph 3, of Annexe 6 of the Dayton Agreements, a second office was opened in Banja Luka (in the Republika Srpska) in June 1996. The Ombudsperson may open other offices wherever he or she considers them necessary.

By 30 April 1997, the Office of the Ombudsperson had recorded 534 applications concerning individual cases, the majority of which concerned problems relating to property and respect for the home.

---

1. On 3 November 1998 the European Court and Commission of Human Rights of the Council of Europe were merged to create a new 'single' Court.

The Ombudsperson decided to initiate inquiries in 27 cases, following preliminary examinations, and in 52 others she asked the Government to take urgent steps. In 34 of these cases, the government has responded favourably to the request.

The Ombudsperson has adopted final reports in 6 cases and has referred 29 to the Chamber of Human Rights. She has also adopted 4 special reports. One of them relates to discrimination concerning the right to access to health to care and in the right to practice one's profession.

After a year in office the present Ombudsperson stated in her first annual report that her role of training local lawyers, alongside that of giving Bosnian citizens confidence in the courts, was as important as her judicial role proper in the establishment of the rule of law.

Reference should also made to the function of the High Representative of the OSCE, who is responsible for promoting respect for human rights and to whom the Ombudsperson can forward a report in the event of a person's or entity's not complying with his or her conclusions or recommendations (Article V. 7 of Annexe 6).

The Chamber of Human Rights

The Chamber comprises fourteen members, of whom four are appointed by the Federation of Bosnia and Herzegovina, two by the Republika Srpska and eight by the Council of Europe's Committee of Ministers. The Chamber meets one week a month in Sarajevo.

The Chamber's decisions are final and binding.

Like the Ombudsperson, the Chamber can ask parties to take urgent steps to protect applicants from actions or decisions which could entail a human rights violation.

The Commission for Displaced Persons and Refugees

In addition to the two judicial bodies, Annexe 7 of the Dayton Agreements established the Commission for Displaced Persons and Refugees. The commission comprises nine members, of whom four are appointed by the Federation of Bosnia and Herzegovina, two by the Republika Srpska, and the other three by the President of the European Court of Human Rights.

The commission took up its functions in November 1996 and between then and late March 1997 it recorded 21 000 complaints concerning property rights. It has offices in Sarajevo, Lukavica and Western Mostar.

The commission has handed down 500 decisions and is now able to deliver 1 000 decisions a month. Although these decisions are final and binding, the commission cannot publish them because the entities are not ready to apply them.

The commission offers applicants four options: to re-establish applicants' property rights as soon as possible; to maintain the rights and rent the property; to annul property transfers made without consent; or to receive compensation for property when the money is available.

A total of 8 211 have chosen the first option, 797 the second, 76 the third, and 4 522 the fourth, while 2 114 have refused all the options.

The commission only had sufficient resources to continue in operation until June 1997. It only received one-sixth of the budget it had requested.

The Constitutional Court

Article VI of the constitution deals with the Constitutional Court of Bosnia and Herzegovina. It comprises nine members, four of whom are chosen by the House of Representatives of the federation and two by the Assembly of the Republika Srpska, the other three, currently Mr Danelius, Sweden, Mr Marko, Austria and Mr Favoreau, France, being chosen by the President of the European Court of Human Rights.

The Constitutional Court has jurisdiction over issues referred by any court in Bosnia and Herzegovina, concerning whether a law, on whose validity its decision depends, is compatible with the constitution and with the Convention for the Protection of Human Rights and Fundamental Freedoms and its protocols.

Article X of the constitution, concerned with constitutional amendments, states that "no amendments to this constitution may eliminate or diminish any of the rights and freedoms referred to in Article II of this constitution or alter the present paragraph".

The institutions of the entities

– The Federation of Bosnia and Herzegovina

The Constitutional Court

The Constitution of the Federation of Bosnia and Herzegovina established a Constitutional Court composed of nine judges: six from the Federation of Bosnia and Herzegovina and three non-citizens of Bosnia and Herzegovina appointed by the President of the International Court of Justice.

The Court was constituted in January 1996. Its main function is to settle disputes between the cantons, between the cantons and the municipalities, between the cantons and the federal government, or between the institutions of the federal government. It can also rule on whether a law or regulation is in compliance with the constitution.

It can only receive references from the President or Vice-President of the federation, the chairs of the cantons or one third of the members of parliament. So far, no references have been made to it.

According to the President of the Constitutional Court, problems are resolved by political rather than judicial means.

The Court of Human Rights

This court is provided for in the Constitution of the Federation of Bosnia and Herzegovina and comprises seven members: three judges from Bosnia and Herzegovina and four members appointed by the Council of Europe's Committee of Ministers in accordance with Resolution (93) 6.

The court has not yet been constituted, since the Committee of Ministers has not so far made the appointments for which it is responsible. This is certainly not because of any negligence on its part. It is probably the outcome of further reflection on the potential conflicts between the case-law of the Court of Human Rights of the Federation of Bosnia and Herzegovina and that of the Chamber of Human Rights of Bosnia and Herzegovina, as noted by the Venice Commission, a consultative body on constitutional law, created within the Council of Europe.

According to the Venice Commission, it can be argued that the Washington Agreement providing for the creation of the Court of Human Rights has been politically (if not legally) superseded by the Dayton Agreements. One can even go further and argue that it would be politically dangerous to create this Court.

Resolution (93) 6 constitutes the legal basis for the appointment of the four judges by the Committee of Ministers.[1] The resolution

1. According to Article 1 of Resolution (93) 6: "At the request of a European non-member state, the Committee of Ministers may, after consulting the European Court and Commission of Human Rights, appoint specially qualified persons to sit on a court or other body responsible for the control of respect for human rights set up by this state within its internal legal system (hereafter called the 'control body')".

refers to a state, and not to an entity succeeding a state. The establishment of a court of human rights for one of the two entities, in this case the Federation of Bosnia and Herzegovina, would thus be a symbolically dangerous gesture, as it could be interpreted as encouraging the separation of the two entities. It would also serve to increase the imbalance between the institutions in the two entities.

The Supreme Court

The Supreme Court also comprises nine judges and can be appealed to by the cantonal courts on issues relating to the constitution, laws and regulations of the federation and other issues which do not fall within the jurisdiction of the Constitutional Court or the Court of Human Rights of the Federation of Bosnia and Herzegovina.

Its decisions are final and binding. It is the highest appeal body of the Federation of Bosnia and Herzegovina.

The Ombudspersons of the Federation of Bosnia and Herzegovina

The three Ombudspersons, Branka Raguz, Vera Jovanović and Esad Muhibić, established under the Washington agreements, were appointed by the OSCE. The next appointments will be made by the State of Bosnia and Herzegovina and should take place in 1998.

Their role is that traditionally associated with an ombudsperson, which is to mediate between citizens and the authorities.

To provide them at least with access to a judicial body with decision-making powers, the state ombudsperson has added an article to her Rules of Procedure enabling the ombudspersons of the Federation of Bosnia and Herzegovina to refer cases to her which she can then refer to the Chamber of Human Rights. These ombudspersons have used this opportunity and have already referred two cases to the chamber, which has declared them admissible.

In their 1995 annual report, the ombudspersons maintained that the authorities were not applying the constitution of the federation, which amounted to a situation in which politics took precedence over the law. In their next report, for the period 1 January to 30 June 1996, the ombudspersons stated that the six months following the signing of the Dayton Agreements had seen no improvement in the constitutional situation while the human rights situation had deteriorated.

In the 1996 annual report, their conclusion was still more pessimistic, maintaining that despite their repeated requests to the institutions concerned to take steps to improve the human rights situation it had in fact worsened.

They concluded that since the September 1996 elections the system had become completely paralysed. The application of the Constitution of the Federation of Bosnia and Herzegovina was a precondition for the application of the Dayton Agreements in the State of Bosnia and Herzegovina. They particularly pointed the finger at the absence of legislation and the state of the judicial system. Many other parties, particularly NGOs, have expressed the same concerns.

– *Republika Srpska*

The Constitutional Court

The Constitutional Court comprises seven members serving a non-renewable eight-year term of office. The President is elected by the National Assembly of the Republika Srpska.

Its task is to review the constitutionality and legality of legislation. Matters can be referred to it by the President of the Republic, the National Assembly or the government. Parliament may authorise other bodies of the entity to refer matters to it. It can also consider matters of constitutionality and legality on its own initiative. Individuals cannot apply to it but it can initiate a constitutional appeal.

The Constitution of the Republika Srpska contains no provisions concerning the status of international human rights instruments in the hierarchy of laws. In principle, the instruments listed in the Dayton Agreements, including the European Convention on Human Rights, should also apply in the Republika Srpska. However, the constitution does not authorise the Constitutional Court to rule on whether legislation is in compliance with these international instruments.

The Supreme Court

The Supreme Court was established in 1992. It protects the rights and interests of all citizens and reviews the legality of decisions. It protects human rights and fundamental freedoms in a practical sense, in the context of civil and criminal cases referred to it.

There is no ombudsperson for the Republika Srpska. The Venice Commission, however, felt that an ombudsperson's office should be established.

The proposal to appoint an ombudsperson for the Republika Srpska is supported by the OSCE, the High Representative of the OSCE and the Republika Srpska itself. It is also included in the programme of priority activities for Bosnia and Herzegovina adopted by the Committee of Ministers.

In April 1997, the United Nations Commission on Human Rights adopted a resolution calling on the authorities of the Republika Srpska to immediately establish institutions for protecting human rights and in particular an ombudsperson for human rights.

Very close attention must be paid to how this is carried out. To maintain a parallel approach between the two entities and ensure his independence, the ombudsperson should be appointed by the OSCE or another international institution, as was the case with the three ombudspersons of the Federation of Bosnia and Herzegovina.

Other forms of protection of human rights

As already noted, the various bodies responsible under the Dayton Agreements for protecting human rights are, to varying extents, operational. However, they can only be effective if the rule of law applies, with institutions that function properly and citizens who have confidence in their legal system.

The institutions of the state

The state institutions of Bosnia and Herzegovina do not function. The collective presidency meets very rarely, even though it was intended to hold weekly meetings. Nor does Parliament sit. As a result, although the Bureau of the Parliamentary Assembly has allocated five seats to the Special Guest delegation of Bosnia and Herzegovina, instead of the three initially provided for, the Parliament was initially unable to appoint its representatives. The appointments were finally made on 30 April 1997.

Legislation, particularly that designed to harmonise national laws with international human rights instruments, has not been passed. The consequences of the absence of property legislation are disastrous.

The police

The police in the federation have been strongly criticised for corruption and incompetence. Yet police co-operation is essential. The International Police Task Force has the task of strengthening the local police and even had its terms of reference widened at the London Conference, but it has been accused of not making full use of this mandate.

It is intended to operate similarly in the Republika Srpska, but for the time being the International Police Task Force is meeting local resistance.

It was planned to establish a joint police force, composed of equal numbers of citizens of the two entities, wearing the same uniforms and driving the same vehicles. This proposal has not yet been implemented.

In addition, 120 specially qualified investigators were to be responsible for examining alleged human rights violations by police officers.

The judiciary

The cantonal courts have primary responsibility for ensuring respect for human rights. However, judges are political appointments.

The refugees return

After four years of war and "ethnic cleansing", there were 4.5 million refugees and displaced persons in the former Yugoslavia – in other words, one-fifth of the population of the Yugoslav Federation in 1991.

General situation in the aftermath of the war

The armed aggression against Slovenia (summer 1991) was too short-lived to give rise to significant refugee movements. In contrast, the conflicts affecting Croatia (from autumn 1991 onwards) and Bosnia and Herzegovina (starting in spring 1992), particularly with the ethnic cleansing methods used largely by the Serb forces in both countries, gave rise to the largest movements of displaced persons and refugees in Europe since the second world war. Throughout the territory of the former Yugoslavia, almost 4 million people have left their homes since the start of the conflict (16% of the pre-war population of 24 million). Only a small number of them have been able to return to their homes since 1991.

Of these movements, 60% (approximately 2.5 million people) stemmed from the war in Bosnia and Herzegovina, and around 20% from the war in Croatia, with 10% being due to repression and poverty in Kosovo and the remainder resulting from insecurity and poverty in Serbia, Montenegro and "the former Yugoslav Republic of Macedonia". Among the almost 4 million people, around 1.6 million (that is, 40%) were displaced persons still living in their original republic. Some 600 000 (that is, 15%) lived in a different republic of the former Yugoslavia from the one where they were living before the war; the number of refugees in other countries, mainly in Europe, reached between 1.4 and 1.8 million (35% to 45%). Within this last category, some 1.1 million individuals were registered, but there were an estimated 300 000 to 700 000 refugees living illegally, or semi-legally, in various states of Europe.

In the summer of 1995, approximately 189 000 people of Serb origin left the former North and South Sectors of the United Nations Protected Area in Croatia ("Krajina") following the Croat army's reconquest of this region.

On 21 November 1995, the leaders of Bosnia and Herzegovina, Croatia and Serbia initialled the General Framework Agreement for Peace in Bosnia and Herzegovina, in Dayton (United States). This was an historic event, with this agreement bringing a comprehensive solution to the war in this country and laying the foundations for stabilisation of the whole region. A series of agreements is appended to the main text, including one covering refugees and displaced persons (Annexe 7).

The situation in Croatia

The number of displaced persons and refugees in Croatia was estimated at 406 000, that is, 9.5% of the total population, including some 190 000 Croats displaced within the country. Croatia's annual expenditure on the refugees was approximately US$ 400 to US$ 500 million a year, of which only US$ 40 million was reimbursed in the form of direct contributions from international bodies or bilateral donors. This international assistance, though significant, was nevertheless absolutely inadequate in the face of such a serious situation. According to Croat sources, Croatia spent over US$ 2 000 million on accommodating refugees and displaced persons.

Croatia took in some 900 000 refugees from Bosnia and Herzegovina in all from the start of the war, most of whom later left for other European countries or returned either to their homes or to other regions of Bosnia and Herzegovina. However, after the war there were around 210 000 refugees from Bosnia and Herzegovina living in Croatia.

At the end of the war some 30 000 Croat citizens from Bosnia and Herzegovina were living in Germany and Sweden, the main host countries, while a further 50 000 Croats are estimated to have taken refuge in other European countries.

The Minister and Head of the Croatian Office for Refugees and Displaced Persons stated that his country was drained and could take no more refugees. After four years, most of the refugees and displaced persons (305 449, or 75%) were accommodated in private homes, while 101 500, or 25%, were in collective accommodation centres (hotels, dormitories, refugee centres, barracks, gymnasia, and so on). Increasing numbers of refugees, however, were being forced to apply for collective accommodation, their host families' resources having been used up.

Evidence was brought to light that the situation was particularly serious in the health and education spheres. As the country was unable to meet medical expenses, refugees' only free entitlement was to primary medical care, with special treatment and hospitalisation authorised only if their lives were in immediate danger. Similarly, while schooling was free for "refugee" children (28 724 such children received schooling from 1994 to 1995, and 2 540 had special tuition in the camps), a large proportion of the children concerned received no education.

Refugee camps after the war : Gaza and Kupljensko

The Gaza refugee camp, at Karlovac, was built with the assistance of the German Government and came into operation in 1993.

Some 2 500 refugees and displaced persons arrived at the camp – 1 500 of whom came from Bosnia and Herzegovina – and they lived in 140 prefabricated units. There were three such camps in Croatia, together with another 150 or so other accommodation centres. The camp gave the impression of being orderly and well organised. There was heating equipment in the "houses", but there being no funds to carry out the necessary repairs, maintenance was difficult. Inactivity appeared to be a major problem, with most of the camp's residents not working. The camp did not take in new refugees, the intention being to repatriate those who were there as soon as the situation allowed.

The situation in the Kupljensko refugee camp, near the town of Vojnić in Croatia, was particularly disturbing. The camp residents came from the region of Velika Kladuša, in Bosnia and Herzegovina, a region under the control of Mr Fikret Abdić until 7 August 1995. Mr Fikret Abdić defied the Bosnian Government by concluding agreements with the Serb forces surrounding the Bihac pocket. Following an offensive by the Croat/Bosnian army, thousands of people left their homes and took refuge in Croatia.

These refugees lived in appalling conditions, often sleeping in vehicles or under trees, sanitation being absolutely inadequate. The humanitarian organisations on the spot, particularly the UNHCR, the ICRC and European Community Task Force, made sterling efforts to help these people. The lives of the most vulnerable people – some 6 000 children, 350 elderly people, almost 1 000 wounded and 200 pregnant women – were, however, clearly at risk. The location of the camp was also completely unsuitable, since it lay in a very damp valley.

The ideal solution to these people's situation was always their return and reconciliation with the population remaining in Velika Kladuša. According to the Mayor of Velika Kladuša, Mr Sefik Stulanović, those refugees who have committed no crimes might return without any fears (he believed that this meant 90% to 95% of them), especially as their homes had not been occupied. At the time of the visit only 3 000 to 4 000 refugees had returned. He said that a small minority, the people who were guilty of crimes, were spreading fear among camp residents in order to prevent them from returning.

The Velika Kladuša authorities made a genuine effort to achieve reconciliation, with a federal police force and an ombudsperson present. Agreement was also reached on deployment of a joint police force (comprising Bosnians, Croats and Turks). Nevertheless, acts of revenge still occured.

The situation in Bosnia and Herzegovina

Situation in early 1996 (before the return of the first refugees)

The population of Bosnia and Herzegovina totalled some 3 million; approximately 80% (2.4 million) of its members having become totally or partially dependent on international humanitarian aid as a result of the conflict. It is estimated that the war displaced over 2 million Bosnians, roughly half of them dispersed inside the country and the remainder in twenty-five receiving countries.

Agreement on Refugees and Displaced Persons (Annexe 7 of the Dayton Agreements)

Under the terms of the Dayton Agreements, "all refugees and displaced persons have the right freely to return to their homes of origin. They are entitled to have restored to them property of which they were deprived as from 1991, and to compensation for any property that cannot be restored."

The agreement adheres to the main principles which the Assembly has always advocated in its texts relating to the situation of refugees and displaced persons in the former Yugoslavia, namely freedom of choice of place of repatriation, prohibition of the forcing of refugees to return to, or remain in, places which are dangerous or lack basic infrastructure, respect for the principle of family reunification, the need to ensure guarantees of safety and human rights for repatriated persons, an amnesty for people accused of crimes other than serious violations of international humanitarian law and common law crimes, prohibition of discrimination in the recruitment sphere, and so on.

The agreement, however, does not mention "voluntary" repatriation, the parties preferring the words "the right freely to return". A warning is needed in this context against any forced return, for the situation on the spot still remains unstable. Similarly, where the agreement emphasises the need for an "early return", this must be orderly, peaceful and gradual. There is a need to respect refugees' wishes and ensure their return in full knowledge of local conditions.

The agreement also provides for the setting up of the Commission on Refugees and Displaced Persons, responsible for determining applications for the return of, or compensation for, immoveable property. Four members of this commission will be appointed by the Federation of Bosnia and Herzegovina, two by the Republic of Serbia ("Republika Srpska") and three (and the Chairman) by the President of the European Court of Human Rights. In this respect, it should be emphasised that Annexe 6 (to the Dayton Agreements) containing the agreement on human rights provides for the Committee of Ministers of the Council of Europe to appoint eight of the fourteen members of the Human Rights Chamber which is to be set up to deal with applications relating to human rights violations in Bosnia and Herzegovina. Furthermore, Annexe 4 (constitution) provides that three judges of the nine-member Constitutional Court shall be selected by the President of the European Court of Human Rights, at least for the initial five-year term. The three cannot be citizens of Bosnia and Herzegovina or any neighbouring state.

Annexe 7 also assigned to the Office of the United Nations High Commissioner for Refugees the task of developing, in close consultation with asylum countries and Parties to the Dayton Agreements, a repatriation plan as part of the implementation of the agreements.

In accordance with its mandate, the UNHCR has drawn up a document entitled *Post-conflict solutions: UNHCR programme in Bosnia and Herzegovina and other countries in the region*, which deals with strategic planning for the return and repatriation of refugees and displaced persons and arrangements for the possible lifting of temporary protection. This text was approved by the participants in the meeting of the Humanitarian Issues Working Group of the International Conference on the Former Yugoslavia held by the UNHCR in Geneva on 16 January 1996.

According to the document, the primary objective of the return and repatriation operation was to ensure that lasting solutions be found for displaced persons through a process of "early, peaceful, orderly and phased return" to a place of their choice (home of origin or elsewhere in Bosnia and Herzegovina). The fundamental human rights of returnees were to be protected and their essential needs provided for. Humanitarian assistance was to continue, at least in the short term, to be phased out as the reconstruction process got under way.

The Office of the United Nations High Commissioner for Refugees likewise formulated a detailed plan of operations for return and repatriation which was discussed and largely approved at a high-level meeting on the implementation of Annexe 7 organised by the UNHCR and hosted by the Norwegian Government on 8 March 1996 in Oslo.

Most returns were anticipated from April to November 1996. As for the displaced persons, four "pilot projects" involving 600 displaced Croat and Muslim families were established (in the municipalities of Travnik, Jajce, Stolac and Bugojno). However, their implementation met with serious difficulties which merely highlighted the complexity of the problems raised by return.

As far as the return of the refugees was concerned, the UNHCR suggested phased repatriation as follows: firstly, repatriation to areas of origin where their ethnic group constituted the majority; secondly, return to and resettlement in new areas where their ethnic group was in the majority; lastly, return to areas of origin where their ethnic group was in the minority.

Return in scheduled phases according to ethnic criteria is, of course, a practical solution, but one which is liable to accentuate the country's ethnic division. Germany, for instance, has expressed reservations about this and announced its intention to apply its own criteria, based on the individual circumstances of the persons concerned rather than on their ethnic ties. The Bosnian Government, for its part, advocates return to the homes of origin.

The UNHCR considered that the movements occurred spontaneously for the most part, in private vehicles or by available public overland transport. In order to encourage this process, the UNHCR produced and distributed information reports giving indications as to the development of security conditions and legislation in various regions. This approach is laudable, since repatriants' access to this kind of information is essential for them to make the repatriation decisions of their own free will.

To meet the immediate needs of reconstruction, the UNHCR set up a Trust Fund for Shelter Materials to enable repatriants to begin their own repairs to their homes. Medium and short-term multilateral finance for reconstruction had to be co-ordinated (and largely provided) by the European Union and the World Bank. At the ministerial conference jointly organised by these two institutions, held in Brussels on 12 and 13 April 1996 with the aim of securing financial commitments for the reconstruction programme, donor nations pledged US$ 1.23 billion for reconstruction. In addition, a United Nations revised consolidated appeal was launched on 1 March 1996 to raise a total of US$ 823.2 million, covering the financial requirements of all United Nations institutions in the five former Yugoslav republics.

Lifting of temporary protection for persons having fled Bosnia and Herzegovina

In early 1996 about a million Bosnians were residing in various European countries, most under temporary protection – a measure adopted from the outset of the conflict in the former Yugoslavia in order to cope with the massive influxes of refugees from the region. Temporary applicability being one of the fundamental characteristics of the measure, the receiving states raised the question whether, after the conclusion of the Dayton Agreements, it would have any further justification.

The official removal of temporary protection was envisaged even before the holding of elections in Bosnia and Herzegovina. In view of the material conditions in the area, however, and the fragility of the peace, this position was altered and the UNHCR would thereafter lift protection strictly depending on certain preconditions:

– the implementation of the military provisions of the Dayton Agreements (which on the whole has proceeded according to the schedule laid down);

– the proclamation of an amnesty – the amnesty law was passed by the Parliament of the Federation of Bosnia and Herzegovina and published in the statute book. The Parliament of the Republika Srpska adopted an amnesty bill;

– the improvement of the security and human rights situation, especially the operation of human rights protection mechanisms. The UNHCR further acknowledged that delays in these areas, and in particular the insufficient deployment of the International Police Task Force, had played a significant part in the Serb population's flight from the districts of Sarajevo which have come under the control of the Federation of Bosnia and Herzegovina.

The UNHCR considered that any untimely return effected in the absence of satisfactory conditions for the reception of the persons concerned would be inhumane towards them and liable to upset the peace process. Nor could trust be restored between the various communities in the space of a few months; consequently, insistence on carrying out repatriation with all possible speed could accentuate the country's ethnic division in that the refugees would rather return to regions under the control of their ethnic group than to their homes of origin.

Germany, which took in some 300 000 Bosnian refugees, ordered the official removal of temporary protection on 1 July 1996. After that date, a return programme was to be commenced. Anyone not abiding by its schedule would be forcibly repatriated.

This position provoked grave concern. In the UNHCR's – and also most other host countries' – opinion, any unilateral measure in this respect could trigger secondary refugee movements between host states. Co-ordination as regards the lifting of temporary protection was therefore an absolute necessity.

In order to help them reach their decision to return, persons under temporary protection should be able to make preparatory "look-and-see visits" to Bosnia and Herzegovina while retaining the right to re-enter the host country. The relevant UNHCR recommendation received a favourable response in the host states.

Refugee voting

Registration for elections, as a token of intended return, expressed a political commitment and not a legal obligation. The number of persons voting from abroad was expected to be large; the UNHCR launched an appeal for receiving states to facilitate *in situ* polling for Bosnian refugees. In addition, travel arrangements would be made for refugees to vote in Bosnia and Herzegovina, with guaranteed return to the host country.

Situation in early 1998

The actual return figures for 1996 and 1997[1] fell short of expectations, as regards both refugees and displaced persons. Moreover, an additional 80 000 people were displaced as a result of the transfer of territories, mainly the Sarajevo suburbs, between the two entities.

At the beginning of 1998, 172 900 refugees returned to Bosnia and Herzegovina (90 000 in 1996 and 82 900 in 1997) mainly from Germany and Switzerland. Over 350 000 refugees had found durable solutions in their host countries: they had been granted a more permanent status, started the process of acquiring citizenship, or obtained it.

Some 689 000 refugees still required a durable solution. The overwhelming majority originated from the minority areas. The greatest number of refugees were located in Germany (approximately 250 000), the Federal Republic of Yugoslavia (253 000) and Croatia (160 000).

Over 204 000 internally displaced people had returned to their homes since the conclusion of the Dayton Agreements (164 000

---

1. All statistics were provided by the UNHCR on 1 July 1997, unless otherwise indicated.

in 1996, 40 000 in 1997), mainly to the Federation of Bosnia and Herzegovina (102 000).

Some 866 000 people remained displaced (450 000 in the Federation of Bosnia and Herzegovina and 416 000 in the Republika Srpska). The majority came from regions where they would now constitute an ethnic minority. They usually occupied the homes of other displaced people or refugees. The inability to find solutions for the displaced through minority returns meant that other return movements were blocked, since the original owners or occupants could not then return to their homes.

In many areas absorption capacity reached breaking point, and new returns, in particular those of ethnic minority groups, resulted in tension and incidents.

Although the UNHCR accepts that refugees originating from majority areas can be expected to return to their homes in those areas, the forced return to majority areas of persons originating from minority areas can only lead to further displacement of the population.

In early 1998 some 600 people were deported (539 from Germany) and thousands were induced to return for fear of being deported. Given the extreme housing shortage in Bosnia and Herzegovina, such practice reduces opportunities for minority returns to take place, since these people usually return to "majority" areas and occupy someone else's house.

The UNHCR is encouraging host countries to implement return policies that have the least destabilising effect on Bosnia and Herzegovina, and enable peaceful, orderly and phased reconstruction of the ethnic composition of the country.

A certain number of "active relocations" (where individuals decide to make a new start in majority areas), as opposed to "passive relocations" (where individuals relocate for lack of an alternative but have no intention to remain) have been observed. Voluntary reversals of war-time shifts of population from villages to cities are, however, difficult to distinguish. The difficult economic situation prevailing in the Republika Srpska may also be a factor discouraging relocations to the Serb majority area.

A separate problem is linked to the presence of 48 000 Croatian Serb refugees, many without identification papers, practically stateless, who settled in the Republika Srpska following operations "Flash" and "Storm", launched by the Croatian Army in the summer of 1995.

Particular attention should be paid to the specific problems encountered by disabled refugees and displaced persons who constitute one of the most vulnerable groups, and in the majority of cases do not enjoy any privileged treatment.

"Majority" returns

By January 1998 returns had occurred mainly to areas where the returnees formed part of the majority group (so-called "majority" returns as opposed to "minority" returns). The great majority of these were to the Federation of Bosnia and Herzegovina.

Most of the majority returns were over by the end of 1996, and this was the main reason for the slower than expected pace of return in 1997.

Up to 80% of these returns were considered by the UNHCR to be "spontaneous", that is, entirely voluntary. A certain number of returns had been "induced" by the threat of deportation, and, as already mentioned, some 600 were actually deported.

The UNHCR's efforts to implement a return plan met with success as far as majority returns were concerned. The authorities in the federation are in principle more co-operative than the authorities in the Republika Srpska, which, for example, have consistently failed to send a representative to attend the Repatriation Working Group. A significant number of the municipal authorities have continuously failed to provide the UNHCR with regular statistics on returnees – figures which are essential to the return and reintegration policy.

"Minority" returns

Almost all displaced persons, and the overwhelming majority of refugees who have not yet found a durable solution, originate from places now under the control of a different ethnic group.

The pace of the return process in this case is visibly slower. In 1996 there were only 10 000 minority returns, most of which occurred discreetly. In 1997 more than 20 000 took place, mainly to the territory of the federation.

Minority returns are still very much blocked. In particular, this is true in regard to the Republika Srpska, the Croat-controlled areas and some hard-line Bosniac areas. The exceptions in the Republika Srpska are some of the Zone of Separation (ZOS) areas and priority areas nominated by the Brèko Return Commission. However, in these cases permanent protection by the Stabilisation Force (Sfor) is necessary in order to allow return in safety. Incidents in some ZOS areas and in Drvar demonstrate that without the security umbrella provided by the Stabilisation Force, minority returns are not possible.

There have also been a small number of minority returns to different locations in the Republika Srpska like Sipovo, Kotor Varos and Banja Luka. But, in general the Government of the Republika Srpska maintains an anti-minority return policy, using the argument that the needs and rights of the displaced Serbs must be met first. There is no possibility for minority returns to the eastern part of the Republika Srpska.

The Croat-controlled areas in southern Bosnia and Herzegovina are particularly hostile to minority returns, although there have been some returns of Bosniacs to Glamoè and to Croat-controlled areas in central Bosnia. They also are dependent on protection by Stabilisation Force troops.

The attitude of the authorities in the federation towards minority returns is, in principle, better than in the Republika Srpska but in many cases, in particular at the municipal level, there is a lot of room for improvement. There are numerous cases of deliberate obstruction and of the application of quotas (exchange of equal numbers of minority returnees between the entities).

It is possible that interest in the UNHCR's "open cities" initiative by local authorities wishing to attract funding will result in a wider opening for minority returns, in particular in Central Bosnia Canton.

Both in the federation and in the Republika Srpska, ethnic groups, in particular displaced persons occupying the houses of minorities, are often manipulated by the nationalist parties to oppose violently the returns of these minority members of a given community.

Measures undertaken to facilitate returns

In order to facilitate the repatriation process in co-ordination with all relevant bodies, the UNHCR initiated the following measures:

• *Simplification of repatriation formalities*

A quintpartite agreement on transit, signed on 29 May 1996 by Austria, Croatia, Germany, Slovenia and Switzerland, has greatly facilitated movements of returnees through the territory of partici-pating states. A number of other asylum states have expressed their interest in acceding to that agreement. The formalities regarding travel documents have also been simplified. However, the consular authorities of Bosnia and Herzegovina are not always capable of streamlining procedures – there are unjustified delays in issuing passports.

- *Repatriation assistance*

Some asylum countries offer different financial incentives which include travel expenses and travel pocket money, a repatriation grant, luggage allowances and assistance to receiving communities. Concern has occasionally been expressed that this might be a source of tension in home communities, but this fear does not seem to be justified. Nevertheless, returnees are often forced to "share" their hard currency benefits through the imposition of high "war taxes".

- *Target areas for return*

In June 1996, the UNHCR initiated a programme aimed at accelerating the return of refugees and internally displaced persons to their original houses through the designation of "target areas", concentrating investment in shelter and infrastructure in order to increase absorption capacity. The International Management Group was entrusted with the leading role in the co-ordination of the programme. The majority of the target areas selected were in the federation (nineteen out of twenty-two at the beginning of 1997), due to the lesser degree of co-operation offered by the authorities in the Republika Srpska. Lack of employment opportunities remained a significant factor constraining the return of displaced people; nevertheless, during 1996 the Target Areas Project made possible the return of more than 100 000 internally displaced persons, mostly to majority areas.

- *Shelter programmes*

In February 1996 the UNHCR initiated the Trust Fund for Shelter Materials in Bosnia and Herzegovina in order to expand its existing shelter material support programme to include urgent repair of housing. The building materials are produced locally in order to increase employment opportunities.

- *Coalition for Return*

Coalition for Return, a multi-ethnic movement of displaced persons from all parts of Bosnia and Herzegovina, was established in October 1996 on the initiative of the Deputy High Representative. Its main aim is to lobby for the creation of an appropriate climate and conditions for return.

- *Community-level confidence building*

This project is carried out under the aegis of the OSCE as part of the long-term democratisation strategy to facilitate the development of a multi-ethnic civil society. The main aim is to develop dialogue and co-operation in areas where the population must overcome mutual distrust. Community-level confidence-building tools include cross-ethnic meetings of all target groups, town meetings, and open information meetings.

The Council of Europe has also elaborated a number of projects for Bosnia and Herzegovina within its general programme of confidence-building measures aimed at increasing tolerance and understanding between peoples. They are carried out in a wide variety of fields, including the media, education, cultural and social areas. Their primary distinguishing characteristic is that the activities involve non-governmental partners. Some of the projects develop the concept of local democracy embassies.

• *Zone of Separation return procedures*

The Zone of Separation (ZOS) is a two-kilometre-wide strip on either side of the inter-entity boundary line and is subject to specific return procedures agreed by the international community in October 1996. Although by the beginning of September 1997, the return applications of some 3 354 families had been approved by the International Housing Commission, only 489 persons had actually been able to do so, mostly to the Republika Srpska side of the Zone of Separation. The main obstacle to return is the very poor security situation and the lack of will to allow people to return to this politically and militarily sensitive area.

Brcko, which is subject to arbitration, is monitored by an international supervisor who has established particular return procedures for this region, allowing some 295 families (1 133 persons) to return to date, under more intense supervision from the Stabilisation Force (Sfor) than in other locations. Only eighty-four families returned in 1996 under the international procedures for return to the Zone of Separation. During the meeting with Ambassador Robert W Farrand, Supervisor, the delegation was informed of specific security problems in this area. The members visited two returnee villages in the Zone of Separation and were able to speak to the inhabitants.

• *Pilot projects within the federation*

Initiated as early as November 1995, this plan originally provided for 600 ethnic minority families to return to "pilot project towns", where confidence-building measures were undertaken. However, the scheme proved to be ineffective, and was not expanded.

• *Assessment visits*

Endorsed by the parties in the joint statement and guidelines of May 1996, these visits unfortunately did not prove to be a success, mainly due to the obstacles created by the local authorities. Nevertheless, the UNHCR continues to support the efforts of leaders of displaced persons and communities seeking to carry out these visits.

- *Transit centres*

Established by the UNHCR jointly with the federation Ministry for Refugees, these centres offer accommodation for returnees for a maximum of forty-eight hours (in practice, much longer) and provide food and other services. The capacity of the centres at the end of 1997 was 3000.

- *Bus services*

In May 1996, the UNHCR introduced the first of eleven (at present) UNHCR-sponsored bus lines across the inter-entity border line to improve and encourage freedom of movement between communities. The bus service allows as many as 5 000 people per week to cross the inter-entity border line.

- *Financial incentives for municipalities*

Municipalities which do not comply with the principles and obligations established by the Dayton Agreement do not receive financial assistance, including reconstruction aid. They are only entitled to humanitarian support. Consequently, the Republika Srpska receives only 2% of financial assistance directed to Bosnia and Herzegovina, and certain municipalities in the federation have been "blacklisted" by the Office of the High Representative (OHR).

- *Open cities*

In March 1997, the United Nations High Commissioner for Refugees launched the Open Cities Initiative aiming at encouraging and rewarding local communities and municipalities which take concrete steps to welcome back previous residents, whatever their ethnic group. Under its Open Cities Initiative, the UNHCR has recognised six open cities in the federation (Konjić, Busovaca, Vogosca, Bihac, Kakanj and Gorazde) and is currently assessing the openness to minority return of twenty-one others.

Obstacles to the return of refugees

- *Housing gap and lack of infrastructure*

The estimated cost for the reconstruction and replacement of damaged and destroyed buildings on the entire territory of Bosnia and Herzegovina is in the order of US$ 1 billion. For the four-year reconstruction programme prepared by the World Bank, the European Commission and the European Bank for Reconstruction and Development, approximately 11.25% has been pledged so far (a total of US$ 450 million). There is a massive shortfall of funding to make housing available for returning and displaced persons. To counter this shortfall, houses are repaired only to such a level as to provide the absolute minimum requirements for human habitation.

There is not enough property to house returnees. Displaced persons are occupying the homes of others. The rate of reconstruction is 30% of the rate of return. In certain regions, particularly in north-eastern Bosnia, and in East Mostar, there is no reception capacity for returnees.

Lack of accommodation is one of the main arguments for municipal authorities to refuse the registration of newly arriving returnees. This creates an additional problem of "unregistered" people, deprived of basic social security. There are no statistics on the number of these people, but in Tuzla alone there are 2 000 to 3 000 Bosniacs from the Republika Srpska without displaced person status.

Although the housing gap affects all returns, the situation is obviously more dramatic when this objective obstacle is compounded by a lack of political will to receive repatriates. Co-operation with municipal authorities and good co-ordination of reconstruction projects are essential.

- *Laws*

The war-time property legislation (laws on abandoned property) regarding socially-owned apartments is still in force. It prevents the return of many pre-war residents, deprived of their accommodation. It is estimated that before the war there were 100 000 socially-owned flats.

The war-time legislation governing privately-owned property has just been amended, but the amendments are not yet in force.

In addition, the civil and military authorities have allocated some "abandoned" property to new residents in contravention of existing provisions.

The Republika Srpska Entity Law on the use of Deserted Property allows for recovery of an occupied property only if the current occupants are able to return to their home in the federation or receive fair compensation. The United Nations High Representative has declared this law a violation of the Dayton Agreements, but it has not been changed so far.

The new provisions of the customs law, which result in refugees no longer being exempt from customs duties on their personal and business possessions, also act as a deterrent to return.

The Amnesty Law in the Republika Srpska has not been amended to cover draft evaders and deserters.

- *Administrative obstacles*

There are various administrative obstacles to return, such as the charging of war taxes and visa and registration fees. As already mentioned, in most areas returnees face serious problems registering with local authorities (in order to acquire social rights and personal documents) if they cannot return to their own homes and have no alternative accommodation, thus creating a large group of displaced people in an irregular situation.

- *Economic situation and unemployment*

Limited employment opportunities constitute a serious obstacle to returns. The unemployment rate is estimated at 52% in the Federation of Bosnia and Herzegovina and 60% in the Republika Srpska. Approximately 80% of returnees do not get jobs on returning. This dramatic situation is combined with ethnic discrimination in the job market.

- *Freedom of movement*

There is still no real freedom of movement between the entities or within the Federation of Bosnia and Herzegovina. This is one of the main impediments to repatriation and return. Restrictions on freedom of movement are largely enforced through an abuse of administrative authority, particularly by the local police. There has still been no real progress in establishing cross-entity postal and telecommunications services, although some cross-entity telephone lines now exist.

The UNHCR therefore fully supports the establishment of a Freedom of Movement Commission. The UNHCR also welcomes the commitment of both entities contained in the joint statement of 21 March 1997 to fully allow safe freedom of movement within the entire territory of Bosnia and Herzegovina.

Both entities have to agree on uniform vehicle registration procedures and the introduction of nation-wide licence plates.

- *Mines*

The presence of mines (estimated at 6 million) is a serious threat to
returnees (as well as, of course, to the entire population). In certain
regions, political will for their removal is clearly lacking, and new
mines have even been laid to deter returnees.

Particular concerns affecting "minority" returns

- *Lack of political will*

The authorities of the Republika Srpska in particular, but also
numerous municipal and cantonal authorities in the Federation of
Bosnia and Herzegovina, are not being very co-operative. The
principle of "reciprocity" is often invoked when refusing reception
of "minority" returns.

- *Lack of security*

The security situation is worrying. There are cases of burning of
houses of potential returnees, as well as of the remining of whole
areas. Crimes committed against members of minority groups are
frequently not investigated and go unpunished. Minority returnees
are harassed and even persons on assessment visits are often met
by groups of protesters who can react violently. If incidents are
fairly rare, that is mainly because minority members avoid taking
the risk of returning.

Secret lists of persons charged with war crimes, targeting minority
groups from a given area, contribute to the fear of return of these
population groups.

The separate police forces in the federation contribute to the climate of insecurity. However, the situation has improved in certain

municipalities in the federation where cantonal police forces have been formed which are composed of joint forces of different ethnic groups.

Relocations

Relocation is still encouraged (and induced) as a means of ethnic engineering. For example, displaced Bosnian Croats are encouraged to live in areas such as Drvar and Glamoè. Displaced Bosnian Serbs in the Republika Srpska are intimidated and harassed by the authorities of the Republika Srpska if they openly consider returning to their own homes in the federation.

The UNHCR is aware of displaced persons, including very vulnerable groups such as mentally handicapped persons, being moved into uninhabitable housing in the Zone of Separation (ZOS) in order to act as a buffer against "minority" returns to this area.

Media propaganda against reintegration

The media are still almost totally controlled by the nationalist parties, particularly in the Republika Srpska and, to a lesser extent, in the Croat-controlled areas. They disseminate anti-return and anti-minority propaganda.

The situation in Serbia[1]

According to the figures of the Office of the Commission for Refugees of the Republic of Serbia, in 1996 the country had 430 000 refugees with regular status and 189 000 people who left the "Krajina" region (Croatia) in August 1995 (and are considered to be "exiles" without refugee status). Among the refugees, 249 000 (57%) come from Bosnia and Herzegovina, 149 000

---

1. 1996 data.

(34.6%) from Croatia and 32 000 (7.6%) from Slovenia. Although refugees of Serb origin are in the majority (324 000, that is, 75.4%), there are also 45 000 "Yugoslav" refugees, 41 000 Muslims and 10 000 Croats.

These people's humanitarian situation was very serious, verging on a humanitarian disaster in the wake of the exodus of Serbs from "Krajina". The humanitarian organisations, together with certain individual states (particularly Russia and Greece) provided some assistance to meet the most urgent needs in terms of food, housing and health care.

In the circumstances, and from the humanitarian viewpoint, the lifting of the sanctions against the Federal Republic of Yugoslavia (Serbia and Montenegro) was welcome as it made it easier to send supplies to the refugees.

Given that the country was virtually drained, it is clear that major humanitarian assistance must continue to go to the most disadvantaged for some time, but the figures available to us at present seem to indicate that only a small minority of the refugees and exiles has shown any desire to return.

This being so, a premature withdrawal of refugee status is inadvisable, since enforced returns on a huge scale might destabilise the fragile balance achieved following the conclusion of the Dayton Agreements. In fact, arbitrary withdrawals of refugee status by the Serb authorities have already occurred at various stages of the conflict in the former Yugoslavia, mainly with a view to keeping the Serb population in regions claimed by the Serb secessionists and to "supplying" soldiers to the latter's forces.

Finally, it is necessary for refugees and exiles in Serbia to be fairly distributed. While the concern to ensure that they are rapidly located in places with an adequate capacity to receive them is understandable, this process may in no circumstances serve as a pretext for changing the demographic balance in certain ethnically mixed regions, such as Vojvodina or Kosovo. Various observers have actually estimated that between 10 000 and 17 000 refugees and exiles have been sent to Kosovo, with more than 60 000 remaining in Vojvodina. Given the existing tensions between Serbs and the minorities in these two regions, the Serbian Government should renounce any attempted alteration of the ethnic balance there and strictly respect the rights of the minorities.

According to the estimates which have been made, of the 1.4 million or so refugees and displaced persons who could opt for resettlement, it is possible that only half would return "home", while the rest would have to be resettled elsewhere. These mass movements of population are on such a scale that planning and general supervision are required to ensure that they are well organised and do not give rise to further conflict. It is also essential for returns to be voluntary and dignified, with human rights and fundamental freedoms being fully respected.

Similarly, a lasting reconciliation will be possible only if the countries concerned enjoy the conditions necessary for sustained economic and social development. Firstly, stricken regions offer no encouragement to people to return and remain, and secondly, an atmosphere of depression and inactivity would lend itself to a resumption of acts of hatred.

Epilogue: a fragile peace

Events in Belgrade in January 1997

Local elections of November 1996

A second round of voting in Serbia's local elections took place on 17 November 1996. The ruling coalition – consisting of Milošević's Socialist Party, the Yugoslav Left, run by Milošević's wife Mirjana Marković, and the New Democracy Party – took control of 154 of 189 municipalities.

A major share of the remaining thirty-five municipalities were, according to provisional results, won by the Zajedno (Together) coalition of three opposition parties: Vuk Drasković's Serbian Renewal Movement, Zoran Djindjić's Democratic Party and the Civic Alliance led by Vesna Pesić.

The extreme nationalist Serbian Radical Party, led by Vojislav Seselj, won the municipality of Zemun, an industrial suburb of Belgrade.

The ruling coalition confirmed the results of the elections to the Federal Assembly held on 3 November 1996, where they won 64 of 138 seats in the Chamber of Citizens. The Zajedno coalition won 22, the Democratic Party of Socialists of Montenegro won 20 seats while the Serbian Radical Party came fourth with 16 seats.

Although the ruling coalition took control of the largest number of municipalities, the opposition won in virtually all major cities in Serbia and Vojvodina.

Following this outcome, courts annulled the elections in fourteen cities,[1] including Belgrade[2] and the second biggest Serbian city, Nis.[3]

Street protests

The decision to annul the opposition victory brought immediate mass protests to the streets of Belgrade and other cities in Serbia. The number of demonstrators varied from 30 000 to reportedly half a million people celebrating the Orthodox New Year on 13 January 1997.

The protests, organised by the Zajedno opposition and by Belgrade students, were characteristically non-violent.

The protestors gained support from a number of Milošević's traditional allies including the Serbian Orthodox Church and the Yugoslav Army. Signs of support also came from Montenegro, where even Milošević's fellow Socialist Party members began to voice doubts about the way in which the situation was handled by the Serbian authorities.

A large riot police force was deployed in a clear attempt to intimidate the demonstrators and prevent the daily street marches. In general, the police were restrained from using force, though there were occasional eruptions of violence with serious casualties[4] as well as reports of arrests and alleged torture of opposition activists.

---

1. Pirot, Draljevo, Uzice, Smederevska Palanka, Vrsac, Soko Banja, Kragujevac, Pancevo, Jagodina, Nis, Zrenjanin, Lapovo, Sabac and Belgrade.

2. Zajedno claimed to have won in 9 of Belgrade's 16 municipalities, which would give them 67 out of 110 seats in Belgrade's City Council.

3. The annulments concerned cities where the opposition won by a narrow margin. In the cities where Zajedno victories were overwhelming – which was the case in Vojvodina's regional capital of Novi Sad – the results were not contested.

4. On 25 December 1996, after clashes between pro and anti-Milošević demonstrators, fifty-six people were treated for injuries, including one man who was shot in the head and critically wounded.

The role of the courts

The provisional election results in the municipalities won by the opposition were contested by the Socialist Party. The decision to annul them was delivered by the municipal courts, usually on the basis of minor procedural deficiencies. This was followed by an administrative and judicial labyrinth of contradictory decisions, involving state-controlled courts and electoral commissions, through which the government repeatedly offered and then withdrew concessions in some of the contested municipalities. The administrative and court procedures seemed to be manipulated in order to buy time, hoping that protests would collapse with time. This practice was strongly condemned by the international community and by a number of Serbian judges.

Political tension in the Federal Republic of Yugoslavia

Following the wave of street protests in November 1996, and under pressure from the international community, the Government of the Federal Republic of Yugoslavia asked the OSCE to send a fact-finding mission. An OSCE delegation, led by former Spanish Prime Minister Felipe González, visited the country and produced a report asking the Yugoslav authorities to immediately recognise opposition victories; enter into dialogue with the opposition; ensure the freedom of the press; recognise and respect the rights of national minorities and abstain from the use of violence against peaceful protests.[1]

Although Belgrade did bow to the pressure and recognised the opposition victories, a report by the OSCE mission observing the Serbian parliamentary and presidential elections in September and

1. In Resolution 1110 (1997) on the situation in the Federal Republic of Yugoslavia, adopted on 29 January 1997, the Assembly endorsed the recommendations made in the González report and called for their full and immediate implementation.

October 1997 concluded that the serious issues raised in the González report remained unresolved.

The parliamentary and presidential elections in Serbia

The parliamentary and presidential elections in September and October 1997 were of crucial importance to Mr Milošević. Unable to serve a third term as the President of Serbia, he decided to continue as the President of the Federal Republic of Yugoslavia and was elected by the federal parliament in July 1997. His grip on power largely depended on the complicity of the republican presidents – both to be re-elected in the months that followed his election.

The parliamentary elections on 21 September 1997

The parliamentary elections held on 21 September 1997 showed declining support for Milošević's Socialist Party. In the coalition with two minor vassal parties it obtained 110 out of 250 seats in the parliament. The lost votes went mostly to Vojislav Seselj's Radical Party who obtained eighty-two mandates. The Zajedno coalition, which combined to win the municipal elections in 1996, fell apart in faction fighting, which all but eliminated any prospects of a democratic alternative. Protesting against the non-implementation of the González recommendations, two of the original three coalition parties boycotted the elections, while Vuk Drasković's Serb Renewal Movement took part and obtained 45 seats. The remaining 13 seats went to 5 minor parties, including those representing ethnic Hungarians from Vojvodina and ethnic Muslims from Sandzak.

The presidential elections on 21 September and 5 October 1997

The first round of the presidential elections took place at the same time as the parliamentary elections, that is on 21 September 1997

The two front runners, Mr Lilić from Milošević's SPO and Mr Seselj, leader of the Serb Radical Party, who obtained 37.6% and 28.5% of votes respectively, went to the second round on 5 October 1997. Mr Drasković came third with 23% of votes.

Mr Seselj reportedly won the largest share of votes in the second round of the presidential elections on 5 October 1997, against Mr Milošević's predecessor as President of the Yugoslav federation, Mr Zoran Lilić. The difference between the two candidates was minimal, with Mr Seselj obtaining 49.18% and Mr Lilić 48.02% of votes cast. However, the elections failed to provide valid results due to insufficient turnout, which was just under the required 50%, at 49.82%.

The re-run of the presidential elections on 7 December 1997

In the first round of the repeated presidential elections, Mr Milutinović came first with 43.7% of votes, the candidate of the Serb Radical Party Mr Seselj came second with 32.19% of votes and Mr Drasković third with 15.42%. Both the candidate of the ruling socialists and Mr Seselj did better than in the invalidated elections in September and October, while Mr Drasković obtained considerably fewer votes than during his first attempt. The turnout was just under 52.75 %. The second round took place on 21 December 1997.

Mr Milutinović won with 59% of the votes, Mr Seselj obtained 37.5% of the votes.

The OSCE described the first round of the presidential elections in Serbia as fundamentally flawed by vote rigging. Their report said the ruling socialists of Slobodan Milošević failed to allow other parties full access to the media or to the vote count. It criticised state media for saying the elections were free and fair, and noted there were worrying irregularities in the southern province of Kosovo, where ethnic Albanians make up 90% of the population.

The presidential elections in Montenegro

The two front runners for the Montenegro presidential elections were the current President – and one of Mr Milošević's closest and most loyal allies – Mr Momir Bulatović, and the Prime Minister, Mr Milo Djukanović, a reformer campaigning for a greater political and economic autonomy of Montenegro. Other candidates were presented by the following parties: the Democratic Party of Socialists, the Group of Citizens, the Fatherland Party, the Serbian Democratic Party and the Party of Natural Law.

The leaders of the six Montenegrin opposition parties signed a declaration on the presidential elections stating that their parties had decided not to take part in the elections. The opposition leaders unanimously stated that the rigid election rules and the political atmosphere would not allow the free and democratic expression of the citizens' will. According to the Montenegrin constitution, each party can have only one presidential candidate. Both the current President, Momir Bulatović, and the Prime Minister, Milo Djukanović, were members of the ruling Democratic Party of Socialists (DPS). Djukanović's faction nominated him for president first and Bulatović was registered as a candidate afterwards. The election commission approved both candidatures; but the Constitutional Court of Montenegro banned Mr Bulatović from standing. Mr Bulatović's options were limited to two – he could either run as an independent candidate or register his faction as a new party. However, on 12 September 1997 the Constitutional Court abolished the limitation of one candidate per party, allowing Mr Bulatović to run as a candidate for the Democratic Party of Socialists (DPS).

The ruling Democratic Party of Socialists split into two factions, one supporting Prime Minister Djukanović and the other President Bulatović. The two men are diametrically opposed over the direction to be taken by Montenegro. Mr Bulatović heads the "conservative" wing, which gives unconditional support to Mr Milošević and calls for an unconditional alliance with Serbia. Mr Djukanović heads a reformist wing and is accused by Belgrade of undermining the unity of the Yugoslavian federation by seeking the "secession" of Montenegro.

Two republics make up the federation: Serbia and Montenegro. The election result might have had serious consequences for Mr Milošević – his grip on power as the President of the federation depends upon the loyalty of the two republican presidents. Montenegro controls half of the upper chamber of the federal parliament, which elects and dismisses the President.

The Speaker of the Montenegrin Parliament invited OSCE monitors to visit Montenegro and observe all the phases of the two-round presidential elections, to take place on 5 and 19 October 1997.

Mr Bulatović came first in the first round with 47.4% while Mr Djukanović obtained 46.7%. The difference between the two candidates was only 2 272 votes, out of 460 568 voters registered for the first round.

On 19 October, Mr Djukanović won the presidential election with 50.8% of votes in the secound round. The defeated candidate, Mr Bulatović, obtained 49.2% of votes. The latter called for the election to be cancelled, alleging numerous irregularities and complained to the Constitutional Court. Almost 10 000 voters registered to vote between the two rounds, mostly young people responding to calls from Mr Djukanović. In addition, the turnout was significantly higher in the second round, 73% compared to 67.5% two weeks earlier.

The monitoring mission of the OSCE did not observe any major irregularities at the election. In its opinion Mr Djukanović's victory reflected the will of the people. According to the US State Department spokesman, there were some irregularities during the election, but they were relatively minor and did not affect the outcome of the voting.

Mr Bulatović's deputies continued to allege that the electoral law and the constitution had been violated. The deputies of the other DPS wing persistently denied such allegations claiming that the elections had taken place in a democratic spirit and that all the rules had been observed.

The Constitutional Court of the Republic of Montenegro, on 27 October 1997, rejected the appeal by Mr Bulatović. Mr Bulatović had claimed that there had been a manipulation of the election register. The court said that, for procedural reasons, it was not in a position to decide on the other parts of the appeal, particularly those relating to the extension of voting at certain polling stations. The legislative committee of the Montenegrin Parliament concluded that there was no constitutional basis for adopting a resolution declaring the results of the presidential elections null and void, as proposed by the deputies of the pro-Bulatović faction of the Democratic Party of Socialists.

Mr Djukanović's victory provoked aggressive reactions in Serbia, particularly from the ruling Socialist Party of Mr Milošević. So far, elections results have not yet been officially recognised. The only high ranking Federal Republic of Yugoslavia official who publicly endorsed the victory of Mr Djukanović was Mr Dunić, the Deputy Prime Minister.

The victory of the coalition supporting President Djukanović in Montenegro created an opportunity for the implementation of democratic reforms in this republic. Their success could have a positive spill-over effect for Serbia. President Djukanović should enjoy the support of the international community provided that he continues to respect his reform commitments. The wide support for the ruling coalition among ethnic Albanians and Muslims in Montenegro is particularly encouraging.

The crisis in Kosovo

Historical context

In 1389, the Ottoman Empire defeated the Serb army in the battle of Kosovo Polje. This marked the beginning of the end of the medieval Serb nation. Serbia was ruled by Ottoman Empire for the next 500 years with Kosovo assuming great symbolic significance in Serbian nationalist history. In 1912 Serbia joined other Balkan states in a war to drive the Ottoman Empire out of Europe and re-acquired Kosovo.

Kosovo is now a region in Serbia in the south of the Federal Republic of Yugoslavia with an overwhelming Albanian-speaking majority (90% of the population). It was given autonomy in the revised Yugoslavian constitution of 1974. The Serbian President, Mr Milošević, took away the province's autonomous status in 1989 and strengthened the Serb presence in the police and armed forces there. He also declared the Albanian language unofficial and changed school curricula. This repression led to a declaration of independence by the Albanian majority in Kosovo, not recognised by the international community, and the creation of an independent parallel government in 1991, with its own institutions to support civil society. Mr Rugova, leader of the Democratic League of Kosovo (LDK), was elected president of the self-proclaimed republic. He advocates peaceful resistance to the Serb authorities.

Tensions have escalated in the last two years since the emergence of the clandestine Kosovo Liberation Army (KLA) in 1996, an armed group that has taken responsibility for a series of violent attacks against Serbian authorities. Some Kosovo Albanians are openly critical of the non-violent tactics of the shadow Albanian administration, as they consider that they have not led to any progress. The actions of the KLA have led to a Serbian police crackdown in Kosovo.

Events in the Drenica region

On 28 February 1998 a unit of the Serbian Ministry of the Interior was ambushed near the village of Likosane, in the Drenica region of Kosovo. Four policemen were killed by members of the Kosovo Liberation Army.

The following day, the Serbian security forces, using armoured vehicles and attack helicopters, swept the area and conducted house-to-house raids. More than twenty people, including ten members of the same family, as well as a pregnant woman, were reported to have been killed over the weekend. Allegedly, some people were killed after having been detained. The Serbian authorities did not acknowledge any civilian casualties, refering to all killed, wounded and detained ethnic Albanians as terrorists.

Mr Milošević stressed that the situation in Kosovo was, and would remain, an internal matter of Serbia.

On Monday 2 March, the Serbian police used truncheons, water cannons and tear gas to disperse about 30 000 ethnic Albanian demonstrators in Priština, protesting against the killings.

In spite of strong international reaction, calling for an immediate end to violence, the Serbian security forces continued their operations in the Drenica region. Two ethnic Albanian villages, Lausha and Donji Prekaz, were attacked at dawn on Thursday 5 March 1998. According to the Serbian Ministry of the Interior some twenty ethnic Albanians, as well as two Serbian policemen, were killed during the operation. Much higher casualty figures of close to one hundred dead, in particular civilians, including children, were later confirmed.

On Sunday 8 March 1998, the Yugoslav authorities announced the end of their security operations. They declared that the presumed leader of the Kosovo Liberation Army, Mr Jashari, had been killed in the assault. They also displayed large amonts of weapons, seized during the operations and allegedly belonging to members of the Kosovo Liberation Army. Serbian officials claim that these weapons had been smuggled from neighbouring Albania.

Reaction of the international community

Immediately after the eruption of violence in Kosovo the international community strongly condemned the indiscriminate and excessive use of force and asked the Yugoslav authorities to put an immediate stop to violence. On 2 March the President of the Assembly called on the authorities to make every effort to de-escalate the situation. She asked the leaders of the Albanian community to condemn and refrain from the use of violence, and called for immediate establishment of dialogue between the two sides. In a letter to the President of the Yugoslav Parliament, Mr Minić, of 4 March the President proposed that a high level Assembly mission visit Belgrade as soon as possible in order to discuss the Kosovo crisis in the context of the relationship between the Council of Europe and the Federal Republic of Yugoslavia.

The meeting of the contact group (9 and 10 March 1998)

On the initiative of the United States and United Kingdom, a ministerial meeting of the six-member (Germany, France, Italy, Russia, United Kingdom and the United States) contact group for the former Yugoslavia was held in London on 9 March. They issued a statement in which they adopted a visa ban on Serbian officials and the halting of government support for trade and investment in Serbia. They urged the United Nations Security Council to impose a total arms embargo on Yugoslavia and to ban the sale of weapons which may be used for repression or terrorism. They threatened to freeze all assets held by the Yugoslav Government abroad if Mr Milošević failed to co-operate. The contact group supported a new mission by Mr González on behalf of the OSCE Chairman-in-Office that would include a new and specific mandate for addressing the problem in Kosovo. They also suggested a role for the United Nations Commissioner for Human Rights to investigate the situation in Kosovo, and urged the International Criminal Tribunal for the former Yugoslavia to consider prosecuting people accused of war crimes in the region.

Russia, which had initially declared its opposition to any punitive measures, finally agreed to some of the sanctions, to be applied during a limited period of time, and did not oppose tothers.

Second meeting of the contact group (25 March 1998)

Following the expiration of the ten-day deadline for compliance with the requests drawn up at the meeting in London on 9 March 1998, the contact group held a second meeting on Kosovo in Bonn on 25 March.

The group noted some progress, notably on dialogue and the implementation of the education agreement, but concluded that further progress was necessary.

It called for a rapid opening of substantive negotiations with the participation of an outside representative or representatives. The group decided to maintain and implement the measures announced on March 9, including seeking adoption of the arms embargo by the United Nations Security Council.

President Milošević was urged to accept the mission of Mr Felipe González, which would open the way to address the potential for participation by the Federal Republic of Yugoslavia in the work of the OSCE.

United Nations Security Council Resolution 1160

On 31 March 1998 the United Nations Security Council adopted Resolution 1160 (1998), banning the sale or supply to the Federal Republic of Yugoslavia of arms and related material. The vote was fourteen in favour to none against, with one abstention by China.

The resolution endorsed the statements made by the contact group on 9 and 25 March 1998 and the decisions of the OSCE Permanent Council of 11 March 1998.

In its resolution the Security Council called upon the Belgrade authorities and the leadership of the Kosovo Albanian community to "enter without preconditions into a meaningful dialogue on political status issues", and expressed support for "an enhanced status for Kosovo, which would include a substantially greater degree of autonomy and meaningful self-administration".

Latest developments in Kosovo and in the Federal Republic of Yugoslavia[1]

Since the outbreak of violence in Kosovo in late February 1998, an estimated 600 to 700 civilians have been killed in the fighting. Some 280 000 people have been displaced from their homes and a considerable number are without any basic accommodation, food or medical assistance.

In July, August and September 1998 the fighting continued, spreading for the first time also to urban areas. In spite of assurances by the federal government that the situation is returning to normal, the evidence on the ground demonstrates the opposite.

1. Data from September 1998.

Units of the Yugoslav army and the Serb security forces continue with operations affecting the civilian population. They are also impeding the access to conflict areas of international observers and humanitarian workers.

In the present situation, it is imperative to create minimum security conditions to allow the return of displaced persons and the beginning of meaningful negotiations on a peaceful solution to the conflict. Such negotiations should also include talks on a future political status for Kosovo.

Security

As the Council of Europe's Parliamentary Assembly has repeatedly stated, the primary responsibility for the violence in Kosovo lies with the authorities of the Federal Republic of Yugoslavia and Serbia. There is abundant evidence of excessive use of force. In addition, numerous allegations of serious crimes committed by the army and the police cannot be fully investigated due to obstruction on the part of the authorities. It is therefore inconceivable that the federal and Serb troops alone could assure the minimum level of security in Kosovo necessary for a genuine peace process to begin.

Armed groups of ethnic Kosovo Albanians are not in a position to guarantee such security either. Their exact numbers, political platform, organisational and command structure are not known. They have also been accused of the killing and abduction of a number of Serb, Kosovo Albanian and Roma civilians. Their presence in the border region with Albania is a further destabilising factor to add to the already volatile situation in this country.

In the circumstances, the deployment of an international peace force, preceded by the withdrawal of the Yugoslav army and the special police troops from Kosovo, followed by disarmament of armed groups of ethnic Albanians seems necessary.

Future political status of Kosovo

The present constitutional framework deprives Kosovo Albanians of the rights they enjoyed before 1990, and has served as a mechanism for their systematic persecution.[1]

An independent Kosovo would have inevitable destabilising consequences for the region. It would, in all likelihood, trigger secessionist demands in "the former Yugoslav Republic of Macedonia" and in Bosnia and Herzegovina. It would also entail the risk of an increase in tensions in Albania, with a negative spill-over effect to other countries in the region.

A future political status for Kosovo should therefore consist of the highest possible level of autonomy for the province, based on the prerogatives the province enjoyed according to the 1974 Constitution of the Socialist Federative Republic of Yugoslavia. These prerogatives should, of course, be adapted to the new situation and, where necessary, enlarged.

The new autonomous status should give Kosovo the right of self-government at the level recognised for the two federal republics. It should also contain the highest possible guarantees for the rights of Serb and other minorities living in Kosovo.

If the new autonomous status of Kosovo as a part of the Federal Republic of Yugoslavia is to be sustainable in the long term, it is necessary that it be co-operative and integrative in nature. It

1. The Council of Europe's Parliamentary Assembly has repeatedly stated that, in its opinion, any future political solution should be based on autonomy for Kosovo, within a democratically reformed Federal Republic of Yugoslavia. It has clearly pronounced itself both against the preservation of the *status quo*, as well as against secession.

should therefore provide for the participation of representatives of non-ethnic Albanian minorities at all levels of the government within Kosovo. It should also provide for the participation of Kosovo representatives in the federal institutions. Without such co-operative and integrative mechanisms autonomy would inevitably lead to Kosovo's political and economic (self) isolation, and finally to secession. It is clear that in the present circumstances co-operation with Belgrade is difficult to conceive. Following the example of Bosnia and Herzegovina, it is clear that considerable pressure would have to be exerted on all parties involved to make it work.

Democratic reforms

A comprehensive programme of democratic reform throughout the Federal Republic of Yugoslavia is another pre-condition for a sustainable long term political solution for Kosovo.

The Kosovo crisis has been used by the present regime of President Milošević as an instrument to seize and maintain power. Tensions have repeatedly been used to consolidate the support, and divert the attention, of public opinion from the political and social problems provoked by the disastrous economic situation and international isolation of the Federal Republic of Yugoslavia. In order to be able to act as a credible partner in a future political solution, Serbia – and the Federal Republic of Yugoslavia – must be democratically reformed to bring the functioning of its political system in line with international standards. Failing that, a repeat of the conflict in the near future will be unavoidable.

The request for immediate democratic changes in the Federal Republic of Yugoslavia is necessary for the legitimacy of the international community's insistence that Kosovo should remain a part of the Federal Republic of Yugoslavia.

In addition, the continuation of the *status quo* not only blocks any long term solution for the crisis in Kosovo, but also carries the risk of the secession of Montenegro, as well as the aggravation of other existing tensions in the Federal Republic of Yugoslavia, such as in Sanjak and, potentially, in Vojvodina.

Finally, the request for democratic reforms should also apply to Kosovo. Its future political status should be based on full respect for Council of Europe standards concerning democracy, the rule of law, human rights and the rights of minorities.

Refugees, asylum seekers and displaced persons

Kosovo

The conflict has resulted in a cumulative displacement of persons. According to the UNHCR there has been a ten-fold increase since spring 1998 in the number of those displaced as well as a sharp rise in the number of those seeking asylum in the immediate region or elsewhere, notably in member states of the European Union. Reliable statistics on displaced persons are difficult to compile owing to the fluid nature of the conflict, and vary from the minimum figure of 290 000, given by the UNHCR, to 400 000 or even 600 000, estimated by the Catholic Relief Services and the Mother Theresa Humanitarian Association.

Thousands of civilians are constantly in flight to escape attacks by government forces. According to UNHCR estimates, there could be over 50 000 displaced people in Kosovo who have been forced to flee from their homes into remote wooded and mountainous areas where they live in the open air or in makeshift shelters. These people are the most vulnerable and are in need of urgent help. Despite assurances from the authorities, access to these areas is hindered, and the immediate priority of humanitarian agencies and non-governmental organisations is to find these groups and to deliver essential relief. It is clear that if these people remain in their current locations over the winter, they will be at serious risk of death. It remains a priority to assist them to return to their homes, or to move them to host families, or, as a last resort, into collective centres where assistance can be more reliably provided.

Due to uncertain access to areas of conflict, humanitarian organisations find it difficult to plan, to estimate needs and to respond quickly with adequate humanitarian aid. In recent weeks, the incidence of cases of restriction of movement and denial of access for humanitarian organisations to certain areas, detention of aid workers and attacks on relief personnel has increased. Oxfam and other humanitarian organisations working in the region have made an appeal to the international community to take political action to ensure minimum security in order to allow humanitarian organisations to work in safety and to protect civilians in zones of conflict in accordance with the Geneva conventions.

An estimated 7 000 to 10 000 homes have been made uninhabitable and many thousands are badly damaged. The great majority of displaced persons are being housed by host families, very often in extremely overcrowded conditions. The Kosovo Albanian community has responded to this crisis with remarkable generosity, but this section of the displaced population is subject to severe problems which will have to be addressed over the next few months.

The municipalities in Kosovo affected by the conflict include Decane, Djakovica, Glogovac, Istok, Klina, Lipljan, Orahovac, Peć, Srbica, Stimlje and Suva Reka. Most of the displaced in Kosovo are staying within these areas, although some have moved to other municipalities. The population in other areas, while not directly involved in the fighting, is increasingly affected by the conflict. Many people have little or no access to food supplies, and medical facilities face major supply problems. Crops could not be harvested this year, the inhabitants of farming villages having fled during the summer months.

In April 1998, the Serbian Government placed an embargo on the importation of thirty-five basic food items to the Kosovo region, which has hindered the work of many humanitarian organisations.

After the meeting between President Yeltsin and President Milošević in June 1998, the Serbian Government adopted a framework programme for the resolution of humanitarian problems in the province of Kosovo. Following this outline programme the Serbian Government established twelve distribution centres for humanitarian aid. The success of these distribution centres will depend on the true willingness of the Serb authorities to provide humanitarian aid without using the centres to impose police or military control over the displaced population. International presence and monitoring at the distribution centres are indispensable.

The authorities of the Federal Republic of Yugoslavia have made a commitment to create conditions propitious to the return of refugees and displaced persons to their homes in Kosovo. However, due to inadequate security conditions and the continued destruction of homes, return to many areas is virtually impossible. There is an urgent need to strengthen the international presence in Kosovo in order to promote safety for returnees and confidence-building between the parties in conflict.

The human rights situation in Kosovo has been marked by widespread violations. The Office of the United Nations High Commissioner for Human Rights has received increasing numbers of reports of people being arbitrarily arrested by the Yugoslav authorities for questioning and kept in pre-trial detention for periods well beyond the legal limit. While most of these people have been arrested in connection with police operations in the field, there is a growing number of cases in which Kosovo Albanian political activists, lawyers, humanitarian workers and medical personnel are being arrested and interrogated by the police. On the other hand, reports that some Serb, Kosovo Albanian and Roma civilians, as well as Serb police officers, have been abducted by armed Kosovo Albanians are an additional cause for concern. Amnesty International has proposed that co-operation should be stepped up between humanitarian organisations and those involved in the monitoring of human rights violations.

International donors have been providing funding for the work of the UNHCR, the World Food Programme (WFP), other international aid agencies and humanitarian non-governmental organisations working in Kosovo and neighbouring regions affected by the conflict. However, the scale of funding is still inadequate to fully respond to the magnitude of the humanitarian crisis. For example, enough food is currently provided for approximately 60 000 to 80 000 people per month, while the needs are four or five times higher. Equally, international and local humanitarian organisations need to increase their co-operation in order to ensure greater use of local aid networks and thus more efficient delivery of relief and assistance.

Montenegro

The Montenegrin Red Cross has registered to date around 44 200 displaced persons from Kosovo, situated mostly in the districts around Ulcinj, Rozaje and Plav. During the month of September 1998 around 3 000 inhabitants of thirteen villages in the area of Rugovska Klisura fled to Rozaje after the deployment of Serb forces in the village of Veliki Stupelj west of Pec.

The Red Cross continues with the registration and distribution of flour, rice, sugar, oil, blankets and mattresses. The UNHCR requested the Republican Commissioner for Refugees to provide a list of buildings that could be rehabilitated quickly since temporary shelter is the greatest problem and needs to be solved urgently.

On 11 September 1998, the Government of Montenegro announced that Montenegro had no real capacity for further acceptance of refugees and internally displaced persons, and consequently closed its border with Kosovo. The Montenegrin authorities have returned a number of displaced persons to Kosovo and expelled 3 000 to Albania. The latter are currently being sheltered in local homes or reception centres in Schkodra. On 12 September 1998, the UNHCR sent a letter to the President of Montenegro urging that the border be reopened.

Local police expressed their concern regarding the intense smuggling activities on the Albanian border and the organised transport of displaced persons across Lake Skadar.

Northern Albania

The conflict in Kosovo led to the first arrival of small numbers of refugees in early March 1998. However, the current major influx of refugees from Kosovo into Albania started at the beginning of June 1998. According to the Albanian authorities, some 15 000 refugees are currently living in eleven districts, notably Tropoja, Durrës and Tirana. Most of them are women and children under the age of 16.

The infrastructure is very poor in northern Albania, where in some districts the refugees from Kosovo represent up to 25% of the population. The lack of running water is a problem throughout Albania and is especially serious in the Tropoje district, where up to 70% of the water supplies is diverted illegally for irrigation. Many refugees are living in uncompleted buildings without water supply. There is a very limited capacity for local families to host refugees without substantial outside assistance. Other reception sites, in the south, are being considered for the relocation of refugees.

The security situation in the entire country remains precarious. Incidents of random violence have been reported throughout the country. Aid agencies continue to be concerned about the potential problem of armed fighters withdrawing into the area occupied by refugees. Border violations have occurred between the Federal Republic of Yugoslavia and Albania causing further political tensions in the region.

"The former Yugoslav Republic of Macedonia"

According to the Ministry of the Interior of "the former Yugoslav Republic of Macedonia", 12 000 "guests" from Kosovo were registered in the period between March and July 1998. The UNHCR office in Priština estimates some 20 000 people from Kosovo to have arrived in the country on tourist visas. Around 2 000 are accommodated privately in the region of Tetovo.

The Macedonian Red Cross branches and other humanitarian organisations are supporting these families with food, toiletries and bedding. The UNHCR is assisting some of the families to obtain visa extensions and to access the country's health care system.

The situation in Kosovo has led to an increase in tensions between the ethnic Albanian and Macedonian communities in "the former Yugoslav Republic of Macedonia".

As a policy, the Government of "the former Yugoslav Republic of Macedonia" has declared that the border with the Federal Republic of Yugoslavia remains open. According to the daily *Nova Makedonija*, control of the border between "the former Yugoslav Republic of Macedonia" and Kosovo will soon be reinforced with four new observation posts, making a total of fourteen observation posts on the borders with Albania and the Federal Republic of Yugoslavia.

Kosovo asylum seekers in other European countries

The number of Kosovo asylum seekers in other European countries is very hard to determine. In January 1996, there were some 340 000 present in the main European countries concerned, namely Germany (230 000), Sweden (60 000), Switzerland (28 000), the Netherlands (15 000), Norway (4 000), Austria (2 000) and Denmark (1 700). Although the numbers declined thereafter as the asylum determination procedure resulted mostly in negative decisions, they have begun to rise again since the start of the crisis in Kosovo. Thus, it is estimated that in the first eight months of 1998 17 728 asylum seekers from the Federal Republic of Yugoslavia arrived in Germany, 8 310 in Switzerland, and 2 800 in Austria. Although asylum statistics are not broken down into ethnic origin, it is generally accepted that some 90% of these are Kosovo Albanians. The Office of the United Nations High Commissioner for Refugees (UNHCR) estimates that the total number of asylum seekers from Kosovo in Council of Europe member states is now 150 000.

Germany is still the country with by far the greatest numbers of asylum seekers. However, the positive recognition rate for asylum applicants from the Federal Republic of Yugoslavia in 1998 is just 2.8%, according to the German authorities. Asylum seekers whose applications are rejected have a right to appeal. If that is turned down, they are given three months in which to leave the country voluntarily. Forced deportation is possible thereafter. There are an estimated 135 000 nationals of the Federal Republic of Yugoslavia subject to repatriation from Germany under the readmission agreement signed between the two countries on 10 October 1996. Of these, some 120 000 are rejected asylum seekers. Some 8 500 of the total have been returned (80% of them Kosovo Albanians) since December 1996 in an ongoing process which had been expected to last until December 1999. However, most Länder have suspended deportations in view of the Kosovo conflict, and those that have not will doubtless be forced to do so since the only carrier authorised for this purpose under the readmission agreement is JAT, the Yugoslav national airline which has just been banned from most European Union countries including Germany.

Switzerland is the European country that hosts the second largest number of asylum seekers from the Federal Republic of Yugoslavia, of whom most are from Kosovo. According to the Swiss authorities, the acceptance rate is 5.6%. According to the Swiss Refugee Council, 1 290 were returned from Switzerland between 1 September 1997 and 11 June 1998 pursuant to the readmission agreement which entered into force on 1 September 1997. On 12 June 1998 the Swiss Government suspended deportations to the Federal Republic of Yugoslavia with the exception of criminals, 113 of whom were returned in July and August.

Reports from the United Kingdom indicate a growing influx of asylum seekers from the Federal Republic of Yugoslavia. A recent survey by the British Refugee Council found that there were at least 4 300 Kosovo asylum seekers in the country. A readmission agreement is being negotiated.

Readmission agreements with the Federal Republic of Yugoslavia are also either under consideration or being negotiated by Austria, Belgium, Denmark, Finland, France, the Netherlands, and Norway. Sweden has already signed and ratified such an agreement.

The position of the humanitarian organisations with regard to the growing numbers of asylum seekers from Kosovo is exemplified by a UNHCR position paper issued on 25 August 1998. This pointed out that "well before the escalation of the violence in early 1988 there was documented repression of Kosovo Albanians and there were documented, serious human rights abuses affecting Kosovo Albanians, on political and ethnic grounds". The note went on to state that ethnically-based persecution of all groups was a growing feature of the present situation, and identified several specific groups at particular risk. Many asylum seekers would qualify for refugee status under the United Nations Convention of 1951. If they did not, they should be accorded leave to stay on humanitarian grounds since they had genuine protection concerns as victims of conflict and violence. Safety within the borders of the Federal Republic was not possible for a large number of those displaced, and a further deterioration of the situation could be expected. In view of these considerations, the UNHCR encouraged asylum countries to receive asylum seekers from Kosovo, to ensure that their protection needs were properly and fairly assessed, and to host them for as long as required. The UNHCR also reiterated its request of 9 March 1998 that rejected asylum seekers from Kosovo should not be deported to the Federal Republic of Yugoslavia, on humanitarian grounds, pending a return to stability.

Reaching an agreement[1]

The offensive of Serb security forces continued throughout August and September 1998. It led to the withdrawal of the Kosovo Liberation Army from all of its previously held strongholds and resulted in a mass exodus of civilians. International governmental and non-governmental observers reported systematic use of violence against civilians and destruction of ethnic Albanian property by the Serbs.

On 23 September 1998 the United Nations Security Council adopted Resolution 1199 (1998), adopted under Chapter VII of the United Nations Charter (collective security). Although not explicitly authorising the use of force against the Federal Republic of Yugoslavia, the United States and its allies interpreted it as a sufficient basis for military action in the case of failure to comply with the resolution.

While the authorisation had already been given to Nato military commanders to carry out air strikes against military installations in the Federal Republic of Yugoslavia, a twelfth-hour agreement was reached between the Special Envoy of United States President

1. In November 1998.

Clinton, Mr Holbrooke, and the Federal Republic of Yugoslavia's President Milošević. The agreement, which was later endorsed by Security Council Resolution 1203 of 24 September 1998, stipulated the withdrawal of part of the Serb security forces from Kosovo and the deployment of 2 000 OSCE observers to verify compliance with the terms of the agreement.

Appendix

Texts on the former Yugoslavia adopted by the Parliamentary Assembly of the Council of Europe

Order No. 154 (1960) – Present situation in Yugoslavia

Recommendation 1070 (1988) – Problems of Yugoslav migrants and the development of relations between Yugoslavia and the Council of Europe

Resolution 925 (1989) – Southern expansion of "Economic Europe" and the integration of Cyprus, Malta, Turkey and Yugoslavia into the European economic space

Resolution 969 (1991) – Crisis in Yugoslavia

Resolution 984 (1992) – Crisis in the former Yugoslavia

Recommendation 1175 (1992) – Situation in Yugoslavia

Recommendation 1176 (1992) – Crisis in Yugoslavia : displaced populations

Recommendation 1198 (1992) – Crisis in the former Yugoslavia

Order No. 473 (1992) – Situation in Yugoslavia

Order No. 483 (1992) – Crisis in the former Yugoslavia

Resolution 994 (1993) – Massive and flagrant violations of human rights in the territory of the former Yugoslavia

Resolution 999 (1993) – Situation in Bosnia-Herzegovina

Resolution 1011 (1993) – Situation of women and children in the former Yugoslavia

Recommendation 1205 (1993) – Situation of refugees and displaced persons in several countries of the former Yugoslavia

Order No. 491 (1993) – Situation of women and children in the former Yugoslavia

Resolution 1019 (1994) – Humanitarian situation and needs of the refugees, displaced persons and other vulnerable groups in the countries of the former Yugoslavia

Resolution 1020 (1994) – Economic consequences and problems for neighbouring countries arising from the implementation of United Nations sanctions against the Federal Republic of Yugoslav (Serbia and Montenegro)

Resolution 1042 (1994) – Deserters and draft resisters from the republics of the former Yugoslavia

Recommendation 1238 (1994) – Situation in Bosnia-Herzegovina

Recommendation 1239 (1994) – Cultural situation in the former Yugoslavia

Order No. 493 (1994) – Economic consequences and problems for neighbouring countries arising from the implementation of United Nations sanctions against the Federal Republic of Yugoslavia (Serbia and Montenegro)

Resolution 1066 (1995) – Situation in some parts of the former Yugoslavia

Resolution 1089 (1996) – Implementation by Croatia of its commitments in the framework of the procedure of accession to the Council of Europe

Recommendation 1287 (1996) – Refugees, displaced persons and reconstruction in certain countries of the former Yugoslavia

Recommendation 1297 (1996) – Implementation of the Dayton Agreements for peace in Bosnia and Herzegovina

Recommendation 1301 (1996) – Civilian aspects of the Dayton and Erdut Agreements

Opinion No. 195 (1996) – Croatia's request for membership of the Council of Europe

Order No. 521 (1996) – Implementation of the Dayton Agreements for peace in Bosnia and Herzegovina

Resolution 1110 (1997) – Situation in the Federal Republic of Yugoslavia

Resolution 1116 (1997) – Implementation of the Dayton Agreements for peace in Bosnia and Herzegovina

Resolution 1130 (1997) – Implementation of the Dayton Agreement for peace in Bosnia and Herzegovina

Recommendation 1337 (1997) – Functioning of the institutions for the protection of human rights in Bosnia and Herzegovina

Resolution 1146 (1998) – Recent developments in the Federal Republic of Yugoslavia and their implications for the Balkan region

Recommendation 1357 (1998) – Bosnia and Herzegovina: return of refugees and displaced persons

Recommendation 1368 (1998) – Latest developments in the Federal Republic of Yugoslavia and the situation in Kosovo

Recommendation 1376 (1998) – Crisis in Kosovo and the situation in the Federal Republic of Yugoslavia

Recommendation 1384 (1998) – Crisis in Kosovo and situation in the Federal Republic of Yugoslavia

Order No. 544 (1998) – Crisis in Kosovo and the situation in the Federal Republic of Yugoslavia

Texts on the former Yugoslavia adopted by the Committee of Ministers of the Council of Europe

Declaration on Yugoslavia (adopted on 5 July 1991)

Declaration on Yugoslavia (adopted on 8 October 1991)

Declaration on the conflict in the former Yugoslavia (adopted on 11 September 1992)

Declaration on the systematic practice of rape in Bosnia and Herzegovina (adopted on 9 December 1992)

Declaration on the rape of women and children on the territory of the former Yugoslavia (adopted on 18 February 1993)

Declaration on Bosnia and Herzegovina (adopted on 14 February 1994)

This publication is based on contributions from the committees of the Parliamentary Assembly:

– Massive and flagrant violations of human rights in the territory of the former Yugoslavia and the creation of a transitional mechanism for the protection of human rights in non-member states of the Council of Europe (report by Mrs Haller, Committee on Legal Affairs and Human Rights, Doc. 6743, 20 January 1993)

– Situation of women and children in the former Yugoslavia (report by Mrs Robert and Mr Daniel, Social, Health and Family Affairs Committee, Doc. 6903, 22 September 1993)

– Economic consequences and problems for neighbouring countries arising from the implementation of United Nations sanctions against the Federal Republic of Yugoslavia (Serbia and Montenegro) (report by Mr Piriński, Committee on Economic Affairs and Development, Doc. 6979, 15 December 1993)

– Situation of the media in the former Yugoslavia (report by Mr Berg and Mr Soell, Committee on Culture and Education, Doc. 6994, 17 January 1994)

– Deserters and draft resisters from the republics of the former Yugoslavia (report by Mr Franck, Committee on Legal Affairs and Human Rights, Doc. 7102, 10 June 1994)

– Deserters and draft resisters from the republics of the former Yugoslavia (opinion by Mr Brito, Committee on Migration, Refugees and Demography, Doc. 7117, 30 June 1994)

– Situation in some parts of the former Yugoslavia (report by Mr Bloetzer, Political Affairs Committee, Doc. 7395, 25 September 1995)

– Situation of refugees and displaced persons in some parts of the former Yugoslavia (opinion by Mr Iwiński, Committee on Migration, Refugees and Demography, Doc. 7397, 25 September 1995)

– Refugees, displaced persons and reconstruction in certain countries of the former Yugoslavia (report by Mrs Robert and Mr Iwiński, Committee on Migration, Refugees and Demography, Doc. 7440, 19 December 1995)

– Refugees, displaced persons and reconstruction in certain countries of the former Yugoslavia (opinion by Mr Bloetzer and Mr Van der Linden, Political Affairs Committee, Doc. 7470, 23 January 1996)

– Refugees, displaced persons and reconstruction in certain countries of the former Yugoslavia (opinion by Mrs Gelderblom-Lankhout, Committee on Legal Affairs and Human Rights, Doc. 7472, 23 January 1996)

– Implementation of the Dayton Agreements for peace in Bosnia-Herzegovina (report by Mr Bloetzer and Mr Van der Linden, Political Affairs Committee, Doc. 7509, 28 March 1996)

– Croatia's request for membership of the Council of Europe (report by Mr Van der Linden, Political Affairs Committee, Doc. 7510, 29 March 1996)

– Implementation of the Dayton Agreements for peace in Bosnia-Herzegovina (contribution by Mr Iwiński, Committee on Migration, Refugees and Demography, Doc. 7524, 18 April 1996)

– Croatia's request for membership of the Council of Europe (opinion by Mr Jansson, Committee on Legal Affairs and Human Rights, Doc. 7533, 23 April 1996)

– Implementation of the Dayton Agreements for Peace in Bosnia-Herzegovina (contribution by Mrs Gelderblom-Lankhout, Political Affairs Committee, Doc. 7536, 24 april 1996)

– Implementation by Croatia of its commitments in the framework of the procedure of accession to the Council of Europe (report by Mr Van der Linden, Political Affairs Committee, Doc. 7569, 27 May 1996)

– Civilian aspects of the Dayton and Erdut Agreements (report by Mr Iwiński, Committee on Migration, Refugees and Demography, Doc. 7588, 25 June 1996)

– Civilian aspects of the Dayton and Erdut Agreements (report by Mrs Verspaget, Committee on Economic Affairs and Development, Doc. 7590, 25 June 1996)

– Elections in Bosnia and Herzegovina (information report by Mrs Gelderblom-Lankhout, *ad hoc* committee, Doc. 7633-Addendum IV, 23 September 1996)

– Situation in the Federal Republic of Yugoslavia (report by Mr Bloetzer and Mr Van der Linden, Political Affairs Committee, Doc. 7744, 28 January, 1997)

– Functioning of the institutions for the protection of human rights in Bosnia and Herzegovina (report by Mrs Gelderblom-Lankhout, Committee on Legal Affairs and Human Rights, Doc. 7833, 18 June 1997)

– Bosnia and Herzegovina: return of refugees and displaced persons (report by Mr Iwiński, Committee on Migration, Refugees and Demography, Doc. 7973, 23 December 1997)

– Recent developments in the Federal Republic of Yugoslavia and their implications for the Balkan region (report by Mr Bársony, Political Affairs Committee, Doc. 7986, 19 January 1998)

– Crisis in Kosovo (report by Mr Bársony, Political Affairs Committee, Doc. 8037, 17 March 1998)

– Latest developments in the Federal Republic of Yugoslavia and the situation in Kosovo (report by Mr Bársony, Political Affairs Committee, Doc. 8082, 21 April 1998)

– Crisis in Kosovo and the situation in the Federal Republic of Yugoslavia (report by Mr Bársony, Mr Bloetzer and Mr Van der Linden, Political Affairs Committee, Doc. 8149, 23 June 1998)

– Crisis in Kosovo and situation in the Federal Republic of Yugoslavia (report by Mr Bársony, Political Affairs Committee, Doc. 8204, 22 September 1998)

– Situation of the Kosovo refugees, asylum seekers and displaced persons (report by Mr Iwiński, Committee on Migration, Refugees and Demography, Doc. 8205, 22 September 1998)

Titles in the same series

Mediterranean strategies (1995)
ISBN 92-871-2667-4

Bridging the gap: the social aspects of the new democracies (1995)
ISBN 92-871-2739-5

The gender perspective (1995)
ISBN 92-871-2822-7

Asylum (1995)
ISBN 92-871-2902-9

The child as citizen (1996)
ISBN 92-871-2994-0

History and its interpretations (1997)
ISBN-871-3225-9

A virtual new world? (1998)
ISBN 92-871-3587-8

Sales agents for publications of the Council of Europe
Agents de vente des publications du Conseil de l'Europe

NETHERLANDS/PAYS-BAS

De Lindeboom Internationale Publikaties b.v.
PO Box 202
NL-7480 AE HAAKSBERGEN
Fax: (31) 53 572 92 96

NORWAY/NORVÈGE

Akademika, A/S Universitetsbokhandel
PO Box 84, Blindern
N-0314 OSLO
Fax: (47) 22 85 30 53

POLAND/POLOGNE

Główna Księgarnia Naukowa im. B. Prusa
Krakowskie Przedmiescie 7
PL-00-068 WARSZAWA
Fax: (48) 22 26 64 49

PORTUGAL

Livraria Portugal
Rua do Carmo, 70
P-1200 LISBOA
Fax: (351) 13 47 02 64

SPAIN/ESPAGNE

Mundi-Prensa Libros SA
Castelló 37, E-28001 MADRID
Fax: (34) 915 75 39 98
E-mail: libreria@mundiprensa.es

SWITZERLAND/SUISSE

Buchhandlung Heinimann & Co.
Kirchgasse 17, CH-8001 ZÜRICH
Fax: (41) 12 51 14 81
BERSY
Route d'Uvrier 15
CH-1958 LIVRIER/SION
Fax: (41) 27 203 73 32

UNITED KINGDOM/ROYAUME-UNI

TSO (formerly HMSO)
51 Nine Elms Lane
GB-LONDON SW8 5DR
Fax: (44) 171 873 82 00
E-mail: denise.perkins@theso.co.uk

**UNITED STATES and CANADA/
ÉTATS-UNIS et CANADA**

Manhattan Publishing Company
468 Albany Post Road
PO Box 850
CROTON-ON-HUDSON, NY 10520, USA
Fax: (1) 914 271 58 56
E-mail: Info@manhattanpublishing.com

STRASBOURG

Librairie Kléber
Palais de l'Europe
F-67075 STRASBOURG Cedex
Fax: +33 (0)3 88 52 91 21

Council of Europe Publishing/Editions du Conseil de l'Europe
Council of Europe/Conseil de l'Europe
F-67075 Strasbourg Cedex
Tel. +33 (0)3 88 41 25 81 – Fax +33 (0)3 88 41 39 10 – E-mail: publishing@coe.fr
Web site: http://book.coe.fr